PARADISE PLUMS AND COCOA BEANS

Schizophrenia and Celia's longing for home

Claudia de Verteuil-Holliday

HEDDON PUBLISHING

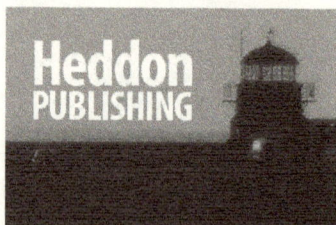

www.heddonpublishing.com
www.facebook.com/heddonpublishing
@PublishHeddon

To the memory of Celia

Celia de Verteuil
Born 13th January 1945 in Trinidad, West Indies
Died 31st May 2012 in Northampton, United Kingdom

The below dates and places outline where Celia spent her life:
1945-1959 Point-a-Pierre then Arima, Trinidad
1959-1981 St Andrew's Hospital, Northampton, UK
1981-1996 St Crispin's Hospital then Moray Lodge, Northampton, UK
1996-2004 St Crispin's Hospital/Princess Marina, Northampton, UK
2004-2012 Lindsay House (NSF), Northampton, UK
2012-2013 Kingsthorpe Grange, Northampton, UK

FOREWORD

The sight of my fourteen-month-old great-niece 'dancing the cocoa' at a Green Market in Santa Cruz, Trinidad, has, in an extraordinary way, linked the past to the present in ways relevant to this work. A photograph of this event, sent to me recently by my sister Rosie, showed the tiny bare feet on the cocoa beans, so clearly identifiable as 'our' feet and at the same time our family origins in Trinidad.

Dancing the cocoa was part of plantation life when I was growing up in Trinidad. After picking, the cocoa beans were laid out on drying sheds in the sun and 'danced' by the estate workers to remove the flesh from the beans and polish them. Sliding roofs covered the beans at night to protect them from damp and rain. Now a part of the heritage industry, it continues to haunt our imagined yesterdays in Trinidad. And what of Paradise Plums? Those pink, lozenge-shaped boiled sweets that we sucked so that they dissolved on the tongue. They too hold a childhood association, for one day, as my sister Rosie and I walked along the shopping area of Frederick Street in Port of Spain, a man called out to us, "Your toes are like Paradise Plums." We knew him to be 'Crazy Arno', a madman to our youthful eyes, who lived on the street, disturbed and untreated like so many others today.

That family footprint in the cocoa connects us to our colonial-Creole past, bringing into focus some of the contextual and psycho-social meanings in this account of my sister Celia's schizophrenia and her longing for home.

Claudia de Verteuil-Holliday

Introduction

Meeting Celia in 1977 was, for me, part of meeting her family. I was soon to marry Claudia and Celia was her sister; the oldest of seven siblings and a still young woman, of the same roots as the woman I was about to marry.

Up to this point I had no direct knowledge of schizophrenia, or of those for whom it formed such an important part of their being. Any idea at all of it was no more than half-formed commonplace assumptions of the condition and an early reading of RD Laing's *Divided Self*. It seemed easy to follow the lazy and reductive language which referred to 'schizophrenics' – "Oh, she's a schizophrenic, I see," as though it was an adequate account or description of a complex, vital woman with a family, a history, a story, a vibrant personality, and a deep and unconditional attachment to Claudia.

Schizophrenia shaped much of Celia's life: where she lived, who she lived with, her diet, even the clothes she wore. However, it neither defined nor encompassed her.

In those early years, and for long afterwards, her sense of self, her identity, was largely constituted through her memories of her early life in Trinidad with her near and extended family. The lengthening years and decades in England were still seen as a necessary but unwelcome interlude. The more powerful reality remained her rootedness in the French Creole life of her childhood: manners, beliefs – especially Catholicism – and the confidence that goes with self-belief.

This became evident as I gradually got to know her through regular visits over a 35-year period. I learned as much about Trinidad and what it was 'to be a de Verteuil' from Celia as from my first visits to the island. I also learned about schizophrenia and the varying, sometimes contradictory, therapies used in its care. From the overtly aggressive electric shock treatment to the ever-evolving pharmaceutical solutions which sometimes seemed as much to do with enforcing quiescent behaviour as alleviating symptoms. 'Cure' as a serious possibility was only rarely raised. Celia endured all this during her long tenure in a variety of institutions with acceptance, revolt, anger and patience.

These qualities are no more representative of psychiatric disorder in Celia than in anyone else. They are the human responses of any fully-formed individual coming to terms with a permanent and devastating deracination. She experienced this trauma as a child, an adolescent, a young woman, through to her old age. Use made it familiar to her and allowed her to integrate it into her life. Not without cost. The feeling of being involuntarily uprooted persisted and would sometimes surface as a momentary melancholy. Cruelly, these occasions were manifest when her schizophrenia was less acute and she was feeling 'better'.

Darker moods did not persist, however. Celia's smile is an enduring memory, as are her – sometimes – homespun reflections on the necessity of the acceptance of one's lot. Whatever she had lost, which was considerable, she retained her Catholic faith as well as a deep affection for, and an absolute trust in, her sister. The strength and power of that aspect of family life did not just endure, but grew over time.

Peter Holliday, Oxfordshire, October 2015

For Celia

I can see her now. A pretty, lively, dark girl. My age, or a year younger, eight or nine at the time, in the yard at Petit Morne Estate. Celia and I are running around with other children; her brother Paul, maybe. We're playing 'kick the pan' or some other form of 'hide and seek' in the late afternoon. The brief dusk of a 1950s West Indian evening declines swiftly into darkness and we have to move to play in the house where our parents are having drinks. Esmé and Peggy de Verteuil, Celia's parents, have come from their estate in Arima to visit my parents on the sugarcane estate outside San Fernando in Trinidad. They are having drinks: rum and sodas or rum punches. We children have Cokes.

It is about six years later that I overhear my mother, to one of my aunts, maybe, saying, "Yes, my dear, she is suffering from religious mania and terrible scruples." I then understand that Celia has to be sent to England, to an asylum.

Peggy, her mother, is distraught. Her father is worried. My parents visit. I go with them to Arima. I also overhear that Peggy, too, suffers from 'religious mania and scruples'.

After that, I heard sporadic accounts from time to time of Celia's life in England. What had happened affected me and I thought about it during my own adolescence. I thought about religious mania and scruples, those obsessive feelings of guilt and shame, which were temporarily allayed by confession and prayers, and seemed to be part of Catholic life for some.

Now, 2015, out of the blue, this account of Celia's life against the background of her family history and a social analysis of Trinidad is sent to me to read by her sister, Claudia. It takes me right back to the Catholicism of the 1950s, and to the white French Creole society in which we grew up, educated by nuns and priests. I feel privileged to have been asked to read this account and I have been moved to tears, but also drawn into its analysis of the diagnosis of Celia's condition as schizophrenia.

Celia's life as told by her sister Claudia is a compelling story, told with sensitivity, understanding and acute insight. It analyses the limitations in mental health diagnoses of the time and the treatments that were then prescribed, drugs and electric shock treatment, with very little or no talk-therapy.

At the heart of this narrative is the voice of Celia herself, through some of her letters to her family; intelligent, with a completely understandable point of view as regards expressing her needs. Her memory of her home, her family and her friends, and the place, Trinidad, are powerful. She so much needed to be fed from there with all the 'fruits' of the place. To have been transported from such a circle of family, cousins and friends into an institution in Northampton is hard to imagine but yet it is glimpsed through Celia's sharp, economic prose. She is, as Claudia says, 'consistently coherent'.

This narrative has achieved a balance between a painful family story and an historical and psychological analysis, asking pertinent questions about our knowledge of schizophrenia and its treatment. It does not seek to blame, but to further our understanding. It is respectful of Celia, her mother and father, and their family, for whom Claudia has written it. She, with her husband Peter, had a 40-year relationship of visiting Celia while she lived in institutional and community care.

Celia's extraordinary life is a timely story to read as we again debate our understanding of mental health and the appropriate care for the mentally ill.

Lawrence Scott, London, 2015

I am

John Clare (1793-1864), Northamptonshire poet
(died in St Andrew's Hospital, Northampton)

I long for scenes where man has never trod;
A place where woman never smil'd or wept;
There to abide with my creator, God,
And sleep as I in childhood sweetly slept:
Untroubling and untroubled where I lie;
The grass below--above the vaulted sky.

Paradise Plums and Cocoa Beans:
Schizophrenia and Celia's Longing for Home

My Life, 1978

I came to England when I was fourteen and my father went to see the best medical supervisor in London, Dr Tennant's father, and he said he would send me to his place and have me well in six months. I've now been here 20 years. I was first in Ward Three and I was very happy there. We were allowed to go to town whenever we wanted and had a cup of tea early in the morning then I went to Robinson Ward. It was alright there and I started to work at the industrial unit and I have worked there for seven years. I worked at the O.T. for quite a long time and I did rugs and trays and odd jobs like washing up and cleaning the lampshades I worked very hard even harder in the industrial unit and Cliftonville. I got the right medication at first then I found it was the wrong one and I found then I wasn't getting enough medication so I had to eat things that helped my health.

I write to my parents and my sister comes to visit me, which pleases me.

The author: Celia Marguerite Anne-Marie de Verteuil

My Life was written by my eldest sister, Celia. In 1958, aged fourteen, she left her family and home in Trinidad, West Indies, to receive treatment in England for schizophrenia. Twenty years later, in her 30s, she wrote *My Life* and sent it to us, her family, in Trinidad. This account was written and sent as one of numerous letters exchanged between us, often on thin blue airmail forms.

My mother would often type her correspondence, with copies kept and archived away. The clicking of the letters on the heavy mechanical typewriter is a sound that returns to me and is reminiscent of that time. The reason that so many of these letters are intact and in my possession is because they were so valued as a link between us, so defining personally and as a family.

Though schizophrenia is not mentioned in *My Life*, Celia did acknowledge that she was ill and needed medication to get better. Her description of routine hospital existence leaves us feeling that she was able to function within it and was happy to be visited by me.

In the 1970s, I had only just begun to visit Celia, having come to England to study in 1972. These visits lasted until her death in 2012 and I was accompanied by my husband Peter on almost every occasion. The relationship between the three of us was long-lasting and sustaining and as important as the letters were at an earlier stage of Celia's life in staying connected as a family.

My Life may lack the passion and texture of her more personal letters to my mother but, as with all the letters included here, it is an integrated part of the story of Celia, her family, and schizophrenia.

Both *My Life* and the letters offered:

1. A channel of communication in a pre-electronic age.
2. A hold on life outside of the total institution for Celia. She was able to engage and connect with us who lived on the 'outside' of her world in the asylum.
3. An insight into Celia's world – a mutual engagement that defined us as a family.

Up until her death in 2012 from cancer, Celia continued to be treated for schizophrenia and was dependent on institutional care. In this sense she never recovered from the illness.

In another sense, our enduring relationship and the acceptance and understanding; both of her schizophrenia and of our own family's mental illness that developed over so many years, offer a version of recovery and hope.

For each individual and family member living with schizophrenia, the experience is unique. What I hope to convey in this work is something of the unique experience of this particular family. If schizophrenia is very much in the foreground as a stigmatising illness, it should be understood here against the background of a white French Creole family spanning both pre- and post-Independence Trinidad. The relationship between the two throws up themes of family and personal identity, guilt, shame and loss. As the author, I rely heavily on the correspondence between mother and daughter and on my own interpretative ability to bring past events and 'memories' to help explain what will never go away.

The experience of living with schizophrenia affects who we are and for this reason it is never entirely forgotten or gone. This work is a way of remembering who we are.

The material has been organised in roughly five sections to help readers navigate their way across time (Celia's lifetime) and into the individual experience of one family - split apart by Celia's departure and by the illness itself, yet remaining connected.

Family: Context and History

Celia's birth on 13th January 1945 in Pointe-a-Pierre, Trinidad, coincided with the closing stages and aftermath of the Second World War. By the time she left for England in 1959, the political landscape was shifting towards Independence for Trinidad, which it gained in 1962.
During this period our mother, Peggy, had two mental breakdowns.
She also had seven children; Celia was the eldest, and six siblings followed. The seventh and last, Geoffrey, was born two years after Celia's departure.
We were a white French Creole family who lived in the countryside. The only reference to the wider political context is from a letter dated September 1962 from my mother to a family friend in England.
She writes that: "Trinidad is all agog with the Independence Celebrations... attended by the Princess Royal and all the visiting dignitaries... I don't know what Princess Mary thought about it all, but people like us, although we took an indirect and restrained part in the celebrations, felt it more as a period of mourning than one of celebration."
(Peggy de Verteuil, 8th September 1962, Arima, Trinidad, W.I.)
While the move to post-colonial society was seen as bringing opportunities for some, it also brought limitations for the members of the French Creole group, rather like when traffic lights change from green to red and it's the turn of the other traffic to pass.
At the time, growing up in that setting, we seemed to be unaffected by the mental breakdown and illness of Celia and our mother. What mattered as much, perhaps in a compensatory way, was a sense of fun; being cared for and belonging to a larger group of cousins and friends who lived close by and with whom we shared so much of our everyday lives and play. It is what 'normalised' mental illness for our family. In retrospect, it is clear that mental illness was part of what defined us.
Other defining characteristics were: the importance and ancestry of the family name - de Verteuil - and being Catholic. The name got you into the Country Club and the other, a place in Heaven. The 'membering' rituals of both include an almost obsessive interest in who 'belonged' (was related) to whom, and the establishing of family roots and reunions in order to maintain family ties. Family and religious identities were mutually re-enforcing, through praying and attending mass together, supported in the

belief of the power of prayer and church ritual to solve problems. Those of African and Indian descent lived among us within clearly defined categories and roles as classmates, servants, workmen, etc. but we knew little about their lives. Our social equals belonged to our 'tribe'. To say somebody was a de Verteuil meant that he belonged and could trace his ancestry to the de Verteuil family.

The mythologising of the family through its noble ancestry handed down through the generations was a way of confirming its higher status on the island and, unintentionally, its link with a plantation economic system that exploited both slave and indentured labour for its prosperity.

"The de Verteuil family was originally from Guyenne in the South West of France, and of ancient nobility. As early as 1080, we hear of a Denis de Verteuil who made a donation to the famous Abbey of Maillezais in the Vendée. By the fourteenth century, the de Verteuils were already rich Merchants owning almost the whole of a section or quartier of the town of Bordeaux. Their military reputation, however, was made in the wars of the 17th, 18th and 19th centuries, and as frequently happens as their valour increased their wealth correspondingly declined." (Fr. A. de Verteuil, 1973:P3)

Paul and Valentine de Verteuil were my paternal grandparents and when some of their descendants met for a family reunion in Trinidad in 1992, Anthony Luengo, married to my first cousin, wrote an account to mark the occasion which is attached in full in the Appendix. This helps to provide both a context for French Creole family life and a celebration of the importance of family and the island of Trinidad, "which has for 200 years provided a geographically defined ground of meaning for the de Verteuils", according to Luengo. It also mentions what he describes as the connection to the "*petite noblesse* in Western France", something that family members draw attention to as an aspect of their heritage. Stories of how French Creoles were able to secure privileges, including the granting of land under the Spanish rulers of Trinidad in the late eighteenth century, adds to this sense of preferment.

The reunion Luengo describes included a number of speeches made by family members, some now long settled in countries far from Trinidad. Despite their 'exile', these speech-makers refer to the importance of their Trinidad connections and recall with nostalgia their childhood experiences on the island. Luengo sees this as a "binding force".

Celia was no less connected to Trinidad in her – forced – exile. Her memories of childhood remained vivid until the last years of her life, as did her desire to return home.

Luengo's discussion of the limited choices for suitable marriage partners among the French Creole community cites Waugh's *A Handful of Dust*, where a young woman complains that there are so few young men available for marriage, that they must be Catholic, from an island family. These endogamous arrangements of small communities may run the risks inherent in limited gene pools, including those of both physical and mental impairment. Luengo goes on to list various family members who had married within the tribe.

His conclusion argues and hopes that "family connections would remain strong even as the Trinidadian context for them becomes increasingly tenuous".

This raises a number of questions for the case of Celia. While Trinidad mattered to Celia, did she matter to it? Did Trinidad reject Celia? In this account of the de Verteuil reunion, there were many references to family members from the past and present, but no mention of Celia as an absent family member. This may seem ungenerous but it also reflects our unease with both mental illness and those who experience it.

Being of 'ancient nobility' and a good Catholic went with the territory of being a good de Verteuil. But what happened when the high ideals associated with it were transgressed or re-constructed in some way? The existence of non-white de Verteuils among the population of Trinidad is a case in point. A useful explanation for this phenomenon was that slaves often adopted their owner's name. In reality, the practice of having another family 'on the (out)side' was not uncommon. These families were often provided for on family plantations but remained 'invisible' to their white relatives. Equally discrediting to the de Verteuils, because of their privileged position in society, would have been mental illness.

The impact of the stigma of mental illness combined with guilt could be, in part, attributed to this link between our family gene history or heredity and the development of mental illness.

Barbara Taylor, in *The Last Asylum*, writes: "Madness touches us all in hidden places; the urge to push it away can be hard to resist."

(Barbara Taylor, The Last Asylum, 2014:p259, Copyright © Barbara Taylor, 2014)

In what ways does mental illness differ from a physical illness? Whatever the answer, a mental illness carries a much greater stigma and what we find is a disparity in health funding, in favour of physical rather than mental health. The thrust of the most recent mental health lobby in the UK parliament is for 'parity of esteem' in order to redress this imbalance in government spending on the two services.

There are cultural and historical considerations that have a bearing on this polarity between physical and mental illness and the associated stigma. Among the rural peasant community in Greece, I know of one case where cancer is considered to be taboo. A particular family will only admit to their family member dying from ingesting toxic wild mushrooms, even though she died 'officially' in hospital from breast cancer.

Even today, AIDS elicits the same stigmatising behaviour as cancer did many years ago. Tuberculosis, on the other hand, was seen as the disease of 'choice' among the well-born in Victorian and Edwardian Britain, conferring a romantic and noble death on its victim. For example, John Keats and opera heroines like Mimi in *La Bohème*. Also, well-born ladies in Victorian times, whose consumption confirmed their status in society.

Susan Sontag's *Illness as Metaphor* examines how illness can stand for something other than itself. How we make sense of illness can change in different contexts of time and space and may be linked to a changing variety of causes.

Hallucinations are not what they used to be. In the past they have been understood as the report of a divine vision, which had the power to bring fame and perhaps fortune to the individual concerned and their locality. A queue might form of those wishing to touch the individual's clothing, receive their blessing, and, eventually, recommend them for sainthood. The North European Enlightenment changed that.

More recently, you would be more likely to be given a prescription for a behaviour-altering tranquilliser or, in some cases, be sectioned under the Mental Health Act for reporting what you had seen or heard.

To the ancient Greeks, hearing the voices of the gods, often through dreams, was indicative of a special relationship with the 'other world'. A routine experience for both Homer and Socrates, who describe their demons in terms of 'inner voices'. The 'visions' of the saints in Christian traditions were not seen as a sign of madness but direct contact with the other world and an opening of the 'doors of perception'. The changes in their role reflected the growing influence of scientific methods in understanding the world and the process of secularisation in the Europe of the nineteenth century. Visions and voices came to be seen as 'mania' rather than contact with the divine.

What science attempts to provide us with is an objective measure of the normative by telling us everything and nothing about what is normal and abnormal. The differences between them – the shades of grey – are less easily defined.

The normative contains both physical and social realities as well as, arguably, religious or spiritual phenomena. Therein lies the paradox. In modern psychiatry, the complex collection of distressing symptoms labelled 'schizophrenia' can be accounted for as a disease, which is organically based and may be treated by medication. Typically, a cocktail of drugs is prescribed to ameliorate the symptoms and signs, which can be varied in type and degree for each person.

In the long-term, often the main beneficiary is the pharmaceutical industry, since, unlike a 'cure', the control of symptoms requires an indefinite continuation of the required dosage; that is, continuous medication. The social and cultural meanings associated with an individual's mental health speak to a different model of mental illness. The requirement here is that, within a therapeutic setting, the patient and their family (as it would have been in our case) would understand themselves more fully through the illness, rather than being stigmatised by it. The process of change and adaptation in this model is grounded in relationships and ways of connecting. It requires time, and an approach to treatment which allows the therapist to be both human and professional. This enables the patient to be understood as an individual rather than a set of symptoms.

Relevant here are the words of a leading psychoanalyst, Thomas Freeman, who joked to another analyst that: "...the difference between ourselves and organically based psychiatrists is that they know what is going on. We haven't the faintest idea, so we have to listen to our patients to see if they can help us!" (Barbara Taylor, *The Last Asylum*, 2014:p88, Copyright © Barbara Taylor, 2014)

Given the polarised worlds of psychiatry and psycho-therapeutic and psychoanalytic traditions, the treatment and care of the mentally ill among us falls short of what it should be. The window of opportunity rests with more dialogue and cooperation between the two professional approaches and traditions. On this point I refer to Barbara Taylor's memoir on madness:

"Even in my worst times the madness waxed and waned, until eventually I discovered its causes and made my peace with them. Today I am no crazier than I need to be – than we all need to be – to negotiate modern

life. But the person I am, I became through my madness: not by 'recovering' from it, which implies a return to a previously healthy state, but by entering into it and travelling to its roots."
(Barbara Taylor, *The Last Asylum*:Pxviii-xix, Copyright © Barbara Taylor, 2014)

You are mad when your family can't cope with you any more.
While I am uncertain as to the origin of this observation, I am sure that it applies in our case. We could not cope with Celia at home with us. By sending her away to the asylum, we hoped that she would recover. It also meant that we could 'manage' by compensating for her loss and ours through prayer and letters. There were also visits and links with the hospital and the various institutions that housed her. The fact that the family were not able to offer her the home life that she at times needed and always longed to return to has left its mark – a significant sadness which connects us to each other and still endures. My nightly protection and comfort until well into adulthood was the chant, "God bless Mummy, Daddy, Celia, Paul, Rosie, Raymond, Andy and Geoff."
Never forgotten and always remembered in our prayers. It was how we managed.

A Tricky Moment

'Been to Northampton' and Care in the Community

It was in the 1980s that Celia left St Andrew's, a large mental hospital in Northampton, to live independently 'in the community'. As a result of government policy at the time to close the large hospitals, many patients were discharged and some were given social housing. Other former residents returned to their families, lived in group homes, or vanished into the netherworld of the urban homeless.

In retrospect, Celia was very lucky to have been accommodated, but her time 'outside' was to be brief and my role in bringing it to an end was pivotal. I needed to find her and take her back to hospital.

When I recounted to a friend at the time just what had happened, she told me to write it down. I did. Now it's thanks to her advice that I am able to recall with greater clarity the events of that morning of 6th September 1985. My feelings of apprehension and dread about the events of that morning have not diminished over the intervening years. The passage of time has not muted them. On the contrary, age and experience have placed them into sharper focus.

***

The words 'she/he has been to Northampton' require context in order to understand that they can stand for mental breakdown. But why the association? Is it perhaps a reference to the Northamptonshire poet John Clare, who spent the latter part of his life at St Andrew's Hospital/Asylum in Northampton? More frivolously, the phrase 'he spent his last years in Northampton' became code in obituaries for those who became mentally ill prior to their death. St Andrew's is the hospital where Celia was a patient from 1959 until the age of 36, in 1981. This link between Northampton and mental illness remains very strong within our family narrative.

The story of my search for Celia began as I boarded the train to Northampton from London Euston. On arrival, I walked to Kettering

Road, on the other side of town from the station. Kettering Road made you aware you were not in the South or the North of England, but in the Midlands. Small, red-brick terraced houses, the shop fronts, the accents and people – reminiscent of a TV soap opera – both familiar and local. What was real about Kettering Road was its proximity to St Andrew's Mental Hospital and the fact that it was often visited by patients, either independently or accompanied by members of staff.

Familiarity with this particular group marks it out in another way. Over the many years that I visited Celia in various settings, my observations confirm that the residents of Northampton are more sensitised and accommodating in their dealings with the mentally ill than in any other place I have visited in the UK. To quote Geoff, a shopkeeper in another part of the town, often visited by Celia for cigarettes, "they [meaning people like her] are much better than the locals." Geoff's relationship to the local white population was not a straightforward matter as he was himself originally from India.

The business at hand made me anxious. Beyond finding Celia, I had no plan. Experience had told me that in the situation I found myself in with her, nothing would be predictable. It was an unsettling time for her. Policy-makers in the UK were insisting that services for the mentally ill should be minimised. The idea was to prevent undue dependency by meeting only the needs the patient was unable to meet through their own efforts. Dependency was associated with long-term effects of institutionalisation and the independence imperative behind the closure of the old asylums. The theme of change and the air of displacement around 'care in the community' was the backdrop at this time.

Both our parents had died in the 1980s and Celia had become less pre-occupied with going home to Trinidad. Formerly, she had visited travel agents in the town in an attempt to book a flight home. Talk of the hospital closure now focused her interest on estate agents and house hunting – what must have seemed, to her, a solution to the question of finding a place to live. These were real people in high street agencies having 'real' conversations with Celia and at some point recognising this other reality of someone who had no experience of life lived outside of the 'total institution' and who had no obvious means of paying for their services.

Social housing in the community was provided and in 1985 Celia left St Crispin's Hospital/Moray Lodge to share a house with another male patient from the same setting.

Many, myself included, were aware of the risks of discharging schizophrenics and other mentally ill people from hospital settings into housing in the towns and cities. There was no evidence that there was quality provision for these people and their complex needs in the community. The status quo was judged by many to be a better alternative to low-cost community care. It is my belief that this turned out to be true in reality, in the short-term, for many patients who could not cope. The support they needed was not there and many returned to hospital within weeks and months.

Initially, the prospects looked good for Celia. In the early weeks, I made a visit and I recall that she was happy as we sat, with her housemate, chatting and drinking tea. Since Celia and her housemate smoked, there was cigarette smoke in the air. Celia's housemate had ownership of the teapot, which was always full. Every week, they were visited by someone from the hospital, mainly to ensure that they had the means to buy food for the week. Presumably, the medication was also managed.

However, with no ward routines and no day centre nearby to attend, I could foresee a problem in how Celia would pass the time. What became a real problem very soon after was the arrival of another male occupant at the house. He was much older than Celia, had a criminal record, and drank heavily. I think that Celia had known him before and, against the wishes of the hospital staff, had allowed him to live with her in the house. He needed somewhere to live and she was totally under his influence by then. Later on, he persuaded her to go and live with him in a hostel for the homeless on the other side of the city, free of any kind of hospital supervision. Celia was then extremely vulnerable in every sense, with no link to the hospital or those who had always been responsible for her care and safety. She had my home telephone number at this time and used to call at all hours of the day and night. She also similarly called Mrs Harding, a friend who visited her regularly and about whom I shall write at greater length.

Increasingly, I became concerned for her safety. The following series of phone conversations, recorded in my diary at the time, give some notion of the events which led up to her return to hospital a month or two later and which prompted me to act:

Celia: *Hello... I am now living somewhere else.*

Me: *Does Lisa* (Celia's key worker at the hospital) *know? Who are you living with?*

Celia: *I am married now... he came in a van... I am not going back.*

Me: *You will have to go back.*
Then a ring and a click, she had put the phone down.

Later,
Mrs Harding: *Do you know where your sister is?*
Me: *Yes, I know, but I feel helpless to do anything about it.*
Mrs Harding: *Well, they* (the local authority) *should not have put her in that house with two men in the first place. They* (the local authority) *seem to forget that she has had more than half her life in a mental hospital.*
Me: *What will happen to her?*
Mrs Harding: *He, the man she says she is married to, is an ex-prisoner, alcoholic and well-known as a 'con-man'.*
Me: *Will I just have to let her go and not see her again?*
Mrs Harding: *You may have to. The mental laws have changed and you can't force people any more. I am being visited by my local policeman tonight because I had my purse stolen. I'll ask him if he knows this man.*

Telephone conversations with members of staff from the hospital and Social Services:
Hospital Staff: *I have tried my best with her. There is nothing that I can do. If Celia does come back to live in the house, she will let him in and the same will happen again.*

Staff at Social Services: *Her social worker is away and I think he's ill.*
Me: *Is he answerable to a senior social worker?*
Staff: *He is not around much anyway.*
Me: *When and where can I reach her social worker?*
Staff: *Call on Monday.*

Another desperate conversation with Celia on the phone late at night:
Celia: *Hello... I am having some trouble in the room. I am frightened. It is over a cigarette.*
Me: *Shall I call the police?*
Celia: *No, he has only just come out of prison.*
Me: *I'll call Lisa.*
Celia: *Yes, call Lisa.*

A Tricky Moment:
'Been to Northampton' and Care in the Community

I telephoned Lisa, who replied that, under the Mental Health Act, there was nothing she could do but try and persuade Celia to come to the hospital to talk.

I felt that time was running out for Celia and that anything could happen so the next morning, 6th September 1985, I took a train to Northampton to find her. As I approached the address I had for her, I could see my sister walking into a shop nearby. I ran after her. She looked well and happy, as if nothing untoward had happened. She talked incessantly about 'Bill' and was buying him a birthday card:

> Celia: *Let's go and have a cup of coffee.*
>
> Me: *Yes, we have a lot of talking to do.*

Her invitation was warm and genuine; my response seemed abrupt, terse and tense. We sat in a café and I talked. I tried to explain my anxiety and concern that if she stayed with this man then I could not help her any more. I let her talk and tried to tell her that he was bad for her: he drank too much, took her money, smashed windows, lied to her; all the things she had told me of on the phone about her time with him. I then said that I had to take her back to the hospital. She showed no resistance to this idea. We walked back to the house. Fortunately, no one was there to stop me. We stood outside with her belongings in ten black rubbish bags and waited for a taxi.

On the journey, I became aware of her looking at me – the look came from her and was not open to interpretation, unambiguously saying 'I hate you'. Several things passed through my mind. Had I over-reacted? The hostel was not that bad. Was this the right thing? For what? Had my personal prejudice come into it? Celia was responsible for her own life, but what did a sense of responsibility mean for someone like her? Perhaps for all concerned a breathing space couldn't be bad, I thought as we approached the hospital and I took her back to the ward.

Celia had experienced a glimpse of independence. It was risky and certainly not perfect. We (her family and carers) needed her in an institution where she would be 'safe', or where we thought she would be safe. It had always been our default position. We felt better with her 'inside'. Her embrace of independent living was childlike – perhaps like the start of the long school holidays – full of anticipation, no constraints, and no responsibilities. There was never any conversation about what she would do all day and how she would manage the responsibilities and demands of living day-to-day in the community.

Paradise Plums and Cocoa Beans:
Schizophrenia and Celia's Longing for Home

***

Care in the community, which was meant to transform lives – Celia's and many others – for the better, had contributed, in Celia's case, to putting her at risk. The effects of her long institutionalisation were obvious from the beginning and had made her a target. Her lack of experience of life outside the total institution and of life skills generally presented many challenges for her. When she did strike up a relationship with a man, it felt to me that he had exploited her situation and that she found the relationship frightening and overwhelming.

There were other occasions when Celia mentioned being taunted by passers-by in the street. It is not uncommon for those who have been institutionalised to have their lives blighted by stigma, abuse, and discrimination. Perhaps because the mentally ill and the insane were 'hidden' from view for so long that they arguably remain the last group to be victimised in this way.

The old asylums are part of mental health history and people who would have been treated for schizophrenia in such institutions are now, in the UK at least, living in the community outside. They are supported (or not) through a network of services provided by the voluntary sector, private companies, and local mental health trusts. This revolution in mental health care in the UK today took place in the years between the 1960s and 1980s. In their foundational phase, the old asylums - many established in the early nineteenth century - aimed to provide sanctuary from the travails and stresses of life. They were to be a place of security and retreat from the world where the mentally afflicted, often the offspring of enlightened physicians seeking to humanise madness, could be treated with humanity. The physicians argued that 'lunatics' were not brutes but sick souls who deserved care and nurture. Good food, fresh air and natural surroundings, as well as creative pursuits, were recommended as part of their treatment.

The asylums, however, soon changed in character. There was increasing demand for them, and, as a result of industrialisation, they were mainly in the large cities and conurbations. What followed was by no means uniform development.

The expansion of the service after the First World War did bring about many reforms, with new treatments and rehabilitation programmes. There was more unlocking of wards and, in some institutions, the revitalisation of what was called 'moral' therapy; in short, a greater respect for the insane, who were seen as individuals. This went hand-in-hand with more psychoanalytically-minded medical staff of the hospitals who introduced psycho-social therapies in conjunction with new symptom-suppressant drugs.

I can remember a period in the 1970s when Celia's treatment became more overtly 'curative'. This meant that she was being 'rehabilitated' for more independent living with 'social' and 'life' skills being the focus of her treatment. It required more staff input, to motivate and encourage her to manage her weekly expenditure and meal preparation. She was also given 'work' experience in the industrial units provided onsite. For a period, there was hope. Celia seemed to be functioning more or less symptom-free. One of her psychiatrists at that time even questioned her original diagnosis of schizophrenia.

There has been, for a long time, a group of psychiatrists whose reluctance to give a diagnosis of schizophrenia is based on the premise that it refers to a cluster of symptoms which may or may not affect patients differently. This viewpoint argues that such a diagnosis (of schizophrenia) is both imprecise and limiting.

While things were going well, Celia travelled independently by train from Northampton to have a short holiday in Weymouth, on the English South coast, with Peter and me. I remember thinking how well she appeared to function outside of the hospital at that time. There was even talk in the air amongst members of the family that Celia should travel to Trinidad for a holiday. This trip home never happened and we can only wonder 'what if?'

On reflection, we, the family, were also caught up in the optimism of a programme aimed at the release of patients from the large mental hospitals and on to 'independent living'. There was always a catch built into the system. The programme was a short-term intervention (albeit targeted and well-resourced) for the long-term mentally ill. Hospitals and Trusts did not (and were not prepared to) invest in such high-input, open-ended care. Rather, what they offered was modelled on the premise that either the patient was able to respond and benefit sufficiently to leave hospital or else fall back into institutional dependency. Celia relapsed not long after the attempt at her 'rehabilitation' and ended up in the latter category, like so many others with schizophrenia and enduring mental illness.

On the face of it, reforms that encourage and support people to manage their conditions and move on to recovery are clearly welcome. But this comes with the caveat that in many cases of severe mental illness, 'recover' means living with a chronic illness. The time-limited 'interventions' to get the mentally ill out of the large hospitals could be seen as a camouflage for a policy of service cutbacks. For many patients like Celia, the reality of this policy was anti-recovery because what they needed was on-going care and support (in or out of hospital), across a range of services, to allow their true independence. The year-on-year cuts in the overall mental healthcare budget have resulted in fewer services.

In discussing this subject of cutting people loose and leaving them to struggle on their own, Barbara Taylor writes:

"... true independence - for everyone, well or ill – is rooted in social connection; without this, it is mere isolation and loneliness. This deep need for connectedness is insufficiently acknowledged through the whole of our society, not just in the case of people with mental disorders... studies of recovery programme outcomes demonstrate very clearly that it is where people feel most strongly supported that the greatest success is achievable. But today people are shunted about from team to team, person to person, with little continuity."

(Barbara Taylor, *The Last Asylum,* 2014: Pp252-253, Copyright © Barbara Taylor, 2014)

On balance, and on the basis of currently available information, my judgement of Celia's care was that it was good enough. There were members of staff who stuck by her in an all-important relational approach in their care of her. Celia benefited hugely from her relationship over a fifteen-year period with Mrs Harding, and over more than three decades of visits from Peter and me. With experience, I grew to understand that the way in which these interactions worked best for Celia was by making one's mind available to her; by really hearing what she said and responding non-judgementally; by suggesting ways to help her manage her difficulties.

To respond to, and assist, another in a caring role, in ways that are appropriate and realistic to them, demands empathy and courage.

"All close relationships trigger powerful emotions whose true origins lie elsewhere, often in childhood. 'Caring' relationships in particular evoke feelings of great intensity... And when the feelings that are aroused are unbearable, as they often are in severe mental illness, this responsibility can be very onerous." (Barbara Taylor, *The Last Asylum*, 2014:pxiv, Copyright © Barbara Taylor, 2014)

The Letters

In 1959, two aunts were to play their role in assisting the departure of Celia from Trinidad and her arrival in England. My father's sister, Rosemarie, accompanied Celia on the BWIA (British West Indian Airways) flight to England. As I remember her, Auntie Rosemarie had many of the qualities suited to this caring role. Despite the demands of her own large family, she always seemed available to engage with us children, growing up as neighbours in the central Trinidadian town of Arima. In general, our relatives did what they could to help my parents. Often, they would have us children to stay for extended periods.

My mother's sister Hélène, who lived in England, agreed to be Celia's guardian when she arrived there; a role that my aunt Hélène continued to fulfil until she was too elderly and I arrived as a student in England and was able to visit Celia myself. The two letters I have chosen to include here further contextualise Celia's leaving and referral to St Andrew's Hospital. The first is from my father and the second from Celia's psychiatrist in Trinidad, a Dr Beaubrun. The letters together form a vivid case history of childhood schizophrenia.

"Childhood schizophrenia, also known as very early onset schizophrenia, is a rare and severe form of the mental disorder. It is defined as schizophrenia that starts in children younger than thirteen years of age (and usually over seven years of age), and apart from age of onset and severity, it is much the same as adult schizophrenia."
(Markus Macgill, *Medical News Today*, 2013)
Given how 'rare' and 'severe' the condition was, Celia's diagnosis of schizophrenia must have come as both a relief and intense pressure at the same time.

My father's letter to Hélène:
Dear Hélène,
My apologies for not writing to you before this, but owing to intense "pressure" on all sides and the speed with which I had to get Celia away...
Celia changed from being a normal healthy and clever child to a problem child shortly after we came to live in Arima – aged 11 – she attended St Joseph's Convent Arima and quite unpredictably one day they asked

21

Peggy to remove her from the school. They said they were incapable of controlling her in class – she was an upsetting influence on the other children, not amenable to discipline, rude and critical of her teachers, making 'monkey' faces in church etc. These apparently were the first symptoms of the schizophrenia which was to develop rapidly soon after.

We then arranged to go to St Joseph's Convent Port of Spain and Eddie and Lillia [uncle and aunt] *very kindly had her stay with them at Stanmore Avenue. The twin ideas behind this move being to separate her from Peggy who was showing signs of acute anxiety and nervous strain – a change of environment and new friends would be a good thing.*

This scheme was not a success as Celia refused to study or to interest herself in anything. She became very unhappy, nervous and scrupulous [sic] *and Lillia took her to see a psychiatrist – Dr Beaubrun of St Ann's Mental Hospital. At this stage, Peggy collapsed with a bad breakdown somewhat similar to the one she had ten years ago when we lived at Pointe-à-Pierre.*

They were both under Dr Beaubrun's care and both being treated at the same time. One was bound to have an effect on the other.

Celia improved noticeably in a few months and this was immediately reflected in Peggy's condition.

It was then arranged to send Celia to the Ursuline Convent in Barbados and I took her over to school there last September. She was perfectly normal and I left her very well and happy as confirmed by letters to us.

Peggy recovered miraculously, she put on weight rapidly, changed her mask of misery to one of radiant happiness. We went to the seaside at Mayaro for a week's holiday.

Two months after (November) I received an urgent telephone call from the Reverend Mother Superior in Barbados informing us that Celia would be coming over to Trinidad in the care of a nun the following day. She had suffered a bad mental breakdown. We were appalled when she stepped off the plane at Piarco on the arm of a nun. She looked a complete wreck: thin, hunched, hair dishevelled and, seemingly, unconscious of her surroundings.

Peggy collapsed immediately and in spite of intermittent periods of rationality, is still in a state of abject depression.

Even though Celia had improved considerably over the past few months, Dr Beaubrun, nonetheless, decided that the mother and daughter should be separated – hence Celia's departure for Northampton. Celia's age is thirteen, an adolescent hurdle over which she is finding it difficult to leap.

I am sure that the treatment at Northampton will help her overcome her difficulties. When you see Lillia and Terry [both aunts] *they will, no doubt, be able to enlarge on this tale of woe and sorrow now extending over two years. However, with every dark cloud there is always a silver lining and the other members of my little family are truly splendid and the citrus crop this coming season looks extremely promising...*
Yours as ever
Esmé de Verteuil

Having to consider both my mother's mental health and Celia's illness, when they would have been inextricably linked, would have posed an unbearable dilemma for my father. Who was it to be: wife or daughter? We can only wonder whether he ever thought of it consciously as a choice. That it was clear that Celia could not be managed at home, and "the speed with which I had to get Celia away", explains the solution as my father would have seen it at the time.

Dr Beaubrun's letter to Dr Davies of the Maudsley Hospital in London:
Dear Dr Davies,
Re: Celia de Verteuil aet 14
The parents of this child have asked me to write to someone in the United Kingdom with a view to having her admitted to an adolescent unity, and I have of course thought of the excellent Bethlem Royal Unit. The purpose of this letter is to ascertain whether admission there would be at all possible and if not whether there is any other suitable institution open to her.
Celia was first referred to me in November 1957, when she was 12 1/2. She had been becoming withdrawn and lacking in confidence and was troubled by many 'scruples'. She was full of guilt feelings and preoccupied with death and sin. She wanted to be a saint, and was over scrupulous. She was also not eating or sleeping well. Thoughts of suicide would come into her head, and she was afraid of going to the bathroom alone. She interpreted these thoughts over which she had no control as sins.
I diagnosed juvenile autism with depression, but though that it might be schizophrenia of early onset. I gave her Chlorpromazine and Drinamyl and she improved remarkably and was sent to school in Barbados, where she broke down again and had to be returned to Trinidad. Since then Celia has improved and relapsed, but has never been really well. She has been treated as an outpatient by me and, when I was away from Trinidad

*on holiday, by my colleague Dr L.F.E. Lewis. She has become frankly
deluded believing that she is pregnant, and that her father has made her
so; the tablets given her by Dr Lewis (Chlorpromazine and Stemetil) were
given to take away her religion; that the cook is practising obeah (a form
of occult magic) on her and a number of other things. Sometimes she
thinks that the devil has made her pregnant. She has become manneristic
and her movements awkward and stilted and there seems little doubt that
she is schizophrenic.*

*Celia's family has a history of manic-depressive illnesses on the maternal
side and I am now treating the mother for a depression, which has tended
to clear up and return. Mother and daughter affect each other adversely
and, in particular, Celia seems to retard her mother's recovery with her
negativism and cruelty to the other children. Her mother tends to feel guilt
for Celia's condition.*

*I now think that admission to an institution is highly desirable for Celia,
but her parents are against her coming to this hospital, one of the reasons
given being that Celia is colour prejudiced. It may, however, become
imperative during the interval before arrangements can be made to get
her abroad.*

*Mr Ray Lange, a friend of Celia's family will be calling on you in London
to discuss this matter. Mr Lange is President of the Trinidad and Tobago
Association for Mental Health and is a prominent businessman in the
community here.*

Yours sincerely
Michael Beaubrun

Celia had been under Dr Beaubrun's care two years before she left for
Northampton. He was a well-respected psychiatrist at the large St Ann's
mental hospital in the north of Trinidad. I did not know St Ann's in the
1950s, but when I visited it on my last trip to Trinidad in 2012, it was the
original early 20th century building. It did not feel at all threatening; quite
the contrary, calm and beautifully situated in the hills outside Port of
Spain. It reminded me of a cocoa estate, with its large saman and poui
trees providing shade as you walked around its many separate pavilions.
(Appendix 2 includes information on the history and design of St Ann's).

In 1957, at the same time that Celia was under Dr Beaubrun's care, as
noted in his letter, he also treated my mother for a mental breakdown. Dr
Beaubrun, now retired, has been a significant figure in the psychiatric
history of three female members of my family. I have no detailed

understanding of their treatment under his care. What I do know suggests that his was a bio-medical response rather than a psycho-therapeutic one. Any psycho-therapeutic attempt to help the family understand and process the meaning of madness and depression for us was absent. Family engagement, now often seen as critical to the recovery process, was not available to us then.

Our mother had the first of two mental breakdowns when Celia was about two-and-a-half to three years old. Depressive episodes were a feature of our mother's life and she was permanently medicated for depression. Today, she would probably have a diagnosis of manic depression or what is more often referred to as bi-polar. I remember clearly the shelf of pills in her bedroom cupboard, plainly visible after climbing up as a child in search of hidden Christmas presents. I was also vaguely aware of the tension between her and my father over the cost and use of the pills (there was no free healthcare for us there at that time). Given the frequency of our mother's depressions, Dad must have questioned their effectiveness more than once.

This backdrop to our family narrative of babies and breakdowns is not unusual. According to a recent research paper cited in the *Guardian* newspaper, as many as one third of all mothers in the UK suffer symptoms of depression linked to their baby's birth, while pregnant and/or during the first four years of a child's life (similar to findings in Australia). So often, what is happening around this time is explained in terms of hormonal imbalance. In practice, such a reductionist view may shift the focus from listening to what mothers have to say to a bio-medical response. While this may be appropriate in particular cases, the overall picture is more complex.

The destructiveness and aggression inherent in the nurturing process should not be under-estimated. After the physical birth comes the psychological birth, requiring the same twisting, turning and struggling in order to grow into a 'self' with a good enough 'fit' with the mother. The psychoanalyst, David Winnicott, in his essay *The Use of an Object* refers to this. An illuminating account of this essay is provided by Barbara Taylor in *The Last Asylum* (2014, Pp:212-214, Copyright © Barbara Taylor, 2014)

Surviving the child's infantile destructiveness and remaining whole oneself is no easy task and is a good reason to support the view that multiple attachments to significant others in the child's life are of benefit to the relationship as a way of giving support and spreading the burden, and thus avoiding the isolation that some women feel at this time.

Women from my mother's generation – brought up in the 1920s and 1930s and bringing up their own families in the 1940s and 1950s – were known to 'just get on with it'.

You just shut up and got on with it.

A template for coping and, for many, surviving the hardships of the years before and during the Second World War, there was seen to be no alternative. Doing anything else would have seemed an indulgence. The unsaid being that if you complained or felt unhappy – particularly around childbirth, that happiest of times – you were a failure. My mother's depressions would only have compounded her known religious scruples and sense of guilt.

This material on mother-infant relationships is interesting as it also reminds me of how little I knew of Celia as a young infant. I cannot recall either of my parents talking about her early years in the way that they would tell stories of the early years of my other siblings. A frequently re-told story concerns my sister Rosie who, at two-and-a-half, clearly caused delight when she was asked by an adult family friend from Germany whether or not she had any "brasiers [sic] and sisters", to which she replied, "I only wear vest and panties."

Dad's comment that Celia was a "perfectly normal child" suggests to me that any 'abnormal' behaviour traits she might have had remained dormant until later on. In any case, no reference is made to them anywhere in the surviving sources. However, I do have some memories of the whisperings around at the time. Mum and Dad were the offspring of first cousins. Our Uncle Louis, whose own son was to develop schizophrenia, had once remarked that my parents' marriage had been slightly frowned upon because they were related. The perceived health risks to any children may have led to a stigmatised marriage. Celia was delivered by forceps, implying a difficult birth. Celia's developing illness may have added to the stigma.

From another source, I heard that Celia may have been assaulted when we moved to Arima, though I do not know by whom, or whether it was sexual.

These whisperings came to me from sources outside the immediate family. The narrative that we grew up with was that our sister was ill and had to go to a hospital in England to get well. She was absent from our young lives but always an invisible presence.

The Letters

***

My memories of Arima are vivid. The fruit trees at the back of the house, I remember clearly. They provided our snacks during the day while we were children: guavas, sweet and smelling of jelly, semi-cooked in the hot sun and tasting like a delicious preserve. Oranges that were not actually orange but green Portugals – those satsumas full with flavour and pips which we spat out at random. Pommeract, that wonderful fruit, so rose-red outside and snow-white inside. The trees at the front of the house were almost all 'Julies', the queen of mangoes. Large and spreading, cool and shady for cultivating anthurium lilies underneath.

Behind the mango trees on the other side of the fence was the bush. Villages not very far away blasted Indian music, both familiar and alien to us. Ma Hari and her buffalo herd routinely stampeded through the surrounding bush, which contained secrets and threats for us. Personal to me was that of being groped uncomfortably by an older cousin while I sat side-saddle on the bar of his bike, riding at high speed into the bush and away from view. The bush held threats of potential violence, rapists and bush fires. It was a source of fantasies and a wonderful, imaginative play space. Caribbean folk tales, Anansi stories, Obeah (black magic) were all contained there. And, of course, wild cashew nuts, collected and roasted in the bush.

Dad always seemed happiest and most relaxed living out in Arima. This was especially noticeable when he had just returned from Port of Spain. A lot of the time, as an estate manager, he worked from home or outside on various estate business. On the other hand, Mum felt limited by a life in Arima. The domestic world, as her sphere of influence, was taken seriously, even when she tried to hide away during a depressive episode. The responsibility for bringing us up as good Catholics was her over-riding concern. Long after I had left home to live in London, I continued to receive moral and religious homilies in the form of cuttings from newspapers, magazines, etc. from her in the post.

"Can you imagine if Peggy [Mum] had had access to the internet and email?" asked my brother Raymond. She would certainly have exploited its potential to 'spread the word'.

***

Dr Beaubrun's diagnosis of juvenile autism with depression, possibly schizophrenia of early onset, undergoes something of a transformation in another report in 1971: "she has a long history of mental disturbance with a diagnosis of schizophrenia and autism as a child".

When she died in May 2012, Celia's death certificate mentioned neither schizophrenia nor autism. Officially, she died of dementia. What mattered was the label. Driven by cause and effect, her illness pointed in one direction: a pathway to mental hospital. Once reduced to a set of symptoms: delusions, hallucinations, paranoia, manneristic traits, the individual is fixed in that story about themselves. That is the danger. But of course it is their courage and resilience that is, in the end, self-defining.

Being described as having infantile autism by the medical profession and of being 'mute' for many months after being admitted to St Andrew's Mental Hospital suggests that Celia's early behaviour was far from what was understood as the norm. Her ability to connect with others was highly disfluent. Yet Dad had written that she was "a perfectly normal healthy child". It is just possible that in the general 'tumbling' of family life, Celia's moods and behaviour in early childhood were not see as a priority. It is unlikely that there would have been sufficient awareness to topicalise child development in the same way as today. However, Celia's later 'schizoid-affective' and psychotic responses of increasing severity would have demanded a more systematic approach. Her sexual fantasies in particular (that our father had made her pregnant) would have been too disturbing to cope with within the family context.

R.D. Laing, the influential psychiatrist, and his collaborator A. Esterson, published *Sanity, Madness and the Family* in the 1960s: a collection of case studies of families of schizophrenics. What they attempted to do was to see the family situation not only from without, but the family as experienced by each of its members from inside.

In the case of Mr and Mrs Abbott and their schizophrenic daughter Maya, what soon became clear from extensive taped interviews with them was just how Maya's parents had failed to acknowledge and validate her comments and experience. Laing's thesis was that schizophrenic experience and behaviour is in some sense intelligible in the light of the process of inter-experience and interactions in families. As far as I understand it, this in no way attempts to identify causes but rather, through its approach, to understand and explain processes which may have outcomes, and which require us to look at the problem differently.

In the case of Mr and Mrs Abbott, their understanding of their daughter's behaviour and her impact on their lives was in terms of her 'illness', but the fact of her illness was not at all clear to Maya who, on the contrary, felt responsible for her own thoughts and actions. They belonged to her and not to the illness.

Maya recounted an episode whereby she was preparing some meat, and her mother was supervising too closely so she turned around and threatened her mother with the knife she was using. Maya said she took responsibility for this, and her action was not a result of hearing any voices.

This episode might have passed unnoticed in many households as an example of unexceptional exasperation between daughter and mother. But Maya was labelled as 'ill' and so whatever she said or did subsequently fitted that account and the supposed 'attack' on her mother precipitated her re-admission to hospital.

What is so instructive about this example is that Maya felt responsible for her actions but, as she says, did not understand why she felt the way she did. This is not unusual for young people. Equally typically, the adults in their lives facilitate self-awareness and personality development. One of the ways in which parents validate their child's experience is through listening to them and recognising that this experience is real and meaningful to the child. The roles of parent and child seem to be in reverse in the case of the Abbotts. Maya had listened to her parents but found what they said confusing and mystifying. At best, a dismissal of her personality and, at worst, a denial of who she was.

It is not difficult to see how Maya would come to doubt the validity of her own thoughts, feelings and suspicions about her parents. Any paranoid 'symptoms' or 'signs' of delusional thoughts she may have had would, in this case and according to Laing, have less to do with a pathological process and more the outcome of her interaction with her parents.

There are moments in all relationships, particularly those between parents and children, when it is just too onerous to bear one's own emotions and that of one's child. We are not uniformly equipped to survive the emotional onslaught of parenthood. Celia's self-realisation, for the most part after she was fourteen, took place outside of the family context and inside the total institution of a mental hospital.

The stigma associated with her illness and its rippling effect on our lives was like holding up a mirror to our family, which we did not want to look into. It reminded us of ourselves, and not the selves we wished to be.

Paradise Plums and Cocoa Beans:
Schizophrenia and Celia's Longing for Home

Stigma and its sister, Shame, place limits on our understanding of Celia and her schizophrenia and, ultimately, of ourselves. To have understood then as we do now that Celia's schizoid defences were part of her way of living in the world would have helped to demystify and de-stigmatise what was in our midst. Further along in time, Celia was no longer the ghost at the feast, but a sister to whom we could relate and who we could enjoy.

The Letters (Leaving Home)

Prior to her move to a school in Barbados, Celia was presenting as a problem child. As often happens in families, our parents were deceased long before I was able to ask them questions for which I have sought answers as an adult. There is much, however, about Celia's early adolescence in our parents' letters, which shows their very real concern about her difficult and problematic behaviour. It was clear that my mother could not cope with her and neither could the different schools that she attended.

It was a period marked by frequent changes for Celia, at a time when she most needed stability in her life. After the move to Arima, Celia started at a convent school but it was not long before the nuns there asked my parents to remove her because of her disruptive and rude behaviour. If the nuns in Arima could not cope with her, she fared no better at the convent in Port of Spain where she was sent to live with an aunt and uncle, "for a change of environment and new friends", according to dad's letter. However, her manifest unhappiness resulted in Auntie Lillia taking her to see Dr Beaubrun. Celia's behaviour at this stage was being understood as pathological and very disturbing. The one positive comment around at this time was that Celia was clever and had a remarkable memory.

Her next move was to the boarding school in Barbados. Soon after her arrival there, she wrote home. The letters clearly show her enjoyment of, and desire to attend, school.

2nd October 1958
Dear Mummy and Daddy,
I like the school very much and I am in form IIB which I find is very easy and hope to be in IIIA next year, we are not having exams at Christmas but at Easter.
We all sleep in one big dormitory and have a lot of fun.
Every afternoon we play games and I am learning tennis.
Tell Muffin and my friends that we are only allowed to write once a month to people besides parents, and we can only go for weekends twice a term and I haven't gone yet.
Good by for now
Celia

Paradise Plums and Cocoa Beans:
Schizophrenia and Celia's Longing for Home

24th October 1958
Dear Mummy and Daddy,
The fair is tomorrow and everybody is excited to be wearing a dress for the first time, and I hope to be taking some pictures there and I am getting ten dollars to spend.
I came second in class in the calling of marks, and Janet came third, but a girl from Barbados called Margaret Rose Murphy came 1st and we are all in Green House so it came first but we did not get a cup.
We had a film shown here called 'Good Queen Bess' it was all about history but nice, and that's all.
Adios for now,
Celia

To what extent Celia was conscious of the fact that she was/had a 'problem' and, to the adults around her, the solution lay in removing her from the family, we shall never know. However, within just a year of her writing those letters, she was on another journey, this time to Northampton.

Leaving home as a rite of passage is not unproblematic. It represents a relationship ruptured; a discontinuation of being sheltered and 'held' by those you love and 'belong' to. Having to leave your family, as in Celia's case, because what separates you is too difficult to manage, adds another dimension. Along with the feelings of homelessness and loss there may have been be a mixture of abandonment and guilt. Perhaps emotional 'armour' would be an appropriate term as it describes a process of protective defences against the painful fallout that such separation can inflict on us. This is not totally at odds with the view of those who believe that sending children away to school, or leaving home as a very young adult, has a positive impact on the development of independence and the ability to cope with life. This view is vigorously disputed on the grounds that it argues for emotional defensiveness rather than emotional 'literacy'. The latter refers to a process of understanding our feelings and those of others so that we are equipped to change and adapt, and sustain meaningful relationships, throughout life.

When my father was a boy, it was common practice for those who could afford it to send their children away to school – either to France or to England. It took several weeks to make the trip by boat, with no prospect of a home visit for months or, more likely, years. This was Dad's fate. He had to return to Trinidad during the Great Depression of the 1930s and was unable to complete his education.

I, along with most of my siblings, left home to study abroad outside of the Caribbean. Three of my brothers were boarders at their secondary school. Like the concerned and caring mother that she was, ours desperately exploited every opportunity to send us abroad to 'expand our horizons', though expressly wanting us to return and set up home near to her. My youngest brother, Geoffrey, described the loneliness he felt, and his fate to live alone with Mum and Dad, as one by one we older siblings flew the nest. The 'empty nest syndrome', as applied to the three of them, adds another dimension to our family story.

The physical separation of families makes staying in touch highly significant. Arguably, letter-writing serves more than one function here. Why were Celia's letters and the correspondence between us such a lifeline? What did they mean to us? They were life-defining in providing a continuity of experience through which we could construct our identities – as a family with Celia and her schizophrenia. Though we never had to experience the full impact of having Celia live at home, through her letters she allowed us to identify with *her* reality and accept the possibility of multiple realities – hers, ours, others'.

The ripples of schizophrenia in the family run wide and deep, affecting many aspects of family life, which is simply too much to bear at times. I believe the letters functioned as a kind of holding mechanism for us. They held us together as a family, but also internally. They made it possible, particularly for my mother and for Celia, to survive the pain of separation. Early on, many of her letters read as typical of any young girl's correspondence with her mother, where leaving home is an issue. What is remarkable is that Celia was at the same time receiving treatment (sometimes highly invasive treatment) for schizophrenia thousands of miles away from home, in a mental hospital. The letters would have allowed her to maintain contact with the world outside of the total institution. Visits from family members and other contacts had an influence but primarily her letter writing was pivotal in the construction of her identity. Her adaptations to the institutional life of the asylum defined her as schizophrenic but through her letters, with very few exceptions, she was the loving daughter and sister of a wider family. Very few of her letters show any signs of illness as presumably when she was experiencing debilitating symptoms, she could not and did not write to us. There are two points to be raised about this. One is that schizophrenia, particularly at the onset, is cyclical. Celia was not 'mad' or 'bad' continuously. The second point is that her multiple identities cohabited the person she was to become. It helps us to appreciate all the more the needs of people with both schizophrenia and other enduring mental illnesses, for respite from the world and for 'asylum' but also the need to belong and connect with others. In terms of services for the mentally ill, it is a difficult balance to get right but we can at least identify the need.

And so to the letters themselves. To what do they speak? For Mum and Dad it is the 'pressure' to get Celia away, even at what must have been a huge financial cost. Clearly from their letters they hoped for a 'cure' for Celia's 'illness' but, equally clearly, were ambivalent about the possibility of her returning to the family. Recommendations from her doctors at St Andrew's were that she would benefit by having her family nearby because of her homesickness (the family were not yet seen to be considered as a necessary support in her recovery). My family's inability to pay for her treatment and care at St Andrew's were beginning to concern the authorities and were a cause of continued anxiety. While Celia did show some 'improvement', the underlying message from the hospital to Mum and Dad was that all that could be hoped for was some relief from the symptoms of her illness. This would partly explain my parents' ambivalence towards bringing her back to Trinidad. We can see, through their letters, how they tried to navigate this minefield of emotion and information, while providing family news of the island and reassurance to Celia at all times.

My mother, in particular, was proactive in trying to establish networks of contacts, through the Catholic Church and by other means, to visit Celia and be a 'link' with the family. Her appeal to Elspeth Orchard, an English friend, to find someone to visit Celia, is straight from the heart. The outcome proved to be highly rewarding for Celia, in the form of Doreen Harding, an ex-psychiatric nurse, who began visiting Celia in the 1960s and became an important link and family friend until her death. Mrs Harding was an intelligent woman, with a warmth and capacity to care for others. Her experience of the psychiatric services in Northampton helped me to find my way around that world as well as to learn how to adapt to those in the hospital and how to talk to Celia at different stages in her illness. She will always be remembered, by the family, as a beacon of light shining in what seemed at times to be a dark, endless tunnel.

42 Allen Road in Northampton comes to mind when I remember Mrs Harding. I began visiting her at her small, red-brick terraced house which she shared with her large, fluffy cat. It was there that I enjoyed cups of

warming tea with her in her front room beside the fire. Her own children had long since grown up and left home. It was with great delight that I learnt her nephew was Ross Daly, a celebrated and gifted musician in the field of Cretan folk music.

I have found many instances in Celia's letters of humour and irony as she comments on the world around her. A world strange and terrifying but with glimmers of comfort. Mostly, her letters are of longing to be at home and in Trinidad. Just the mention of fruit: "mangoes, pawpaws, topitambo, portugals and grapefruit" in her letters summed up all her needs to be there and helped to give her correspondence a texture and direct appeal which still resonates with us today.

So much more than pieces of paper, the letters which follow act as a personal and family archive. They contain and generate the thoughts and feelings of a family surviving schizophrenia over several decades. This is the reason why I still have those letters and why it is so difficult for me to consign them to the recycling bin. Better that they are 'recycled' for what they mean and to further our understanding of what it is to live with schizophrenia.

My cousin Muffin wrote to me recently about Celia's departure:

Celia, Pat and I [all cousins)] *were the same age, within a few months of each other. We used to be a threesome together in Arima, and, I am sure, earlier on in Port of Spain and in Cascade, but my memory doesn't go there. I remember curls, olive skin, wide-set eyes, a lovely smile inherited from Auntie Peggy* [our mother], *and energy. And then we all separated; Pat to the USA for school and me to the UK, this was around 1957 or so and we were twelve. Lou was sixteen. It was not long after that Celia was brought to England by Mummy, who had the advantage of a free airfare through Dad who was still at BWIA. This was a time when overseas travel was much more expensive than it is now. She had the heart-breaking task of leaving Celia behind in an English mental hospital where she could get the care she needed for her rapidly developing schizophrenia, a hard cross to bear.*

(Elizabeth (Muffin) Topp neé Cadiz)

Paradise Plums and Cocoa Beans:
Schizophrenia and Celia's Longing for Home

In the months after that BWIA flight, Celia wrote home:

30th September 1959
Dear Mum and Dad,
I am very well and hoping to see auntie Hélène soon.
Please may I have my ears pierced?
Send my earrings, the ones I got at Elena's wedding. My gold bracelets.
My watch if it is fixed and my gold chain, my gold-plated brooch and my
silver charm bracelet and leave the rest to Claudia and Rosie and my
missal and silver chaplet.
Give everyone my love. I hope you're all having a good time. I am.
Love
Celia

November 1959
Dear Mummy,
I am very much better and want to go to school at Notre Dame convent,
Lingfield, Surrey, England.
I am going to PT tomorrow.
We have a nice time here sometimes, giggling and the rest of it.
I have met a very nice lady here called Molly Alexander, she is most nice
and kind to me.
Tell me how the children are getting on at school, I am longing to hear
from them and see them again.
I hope I am not costing you too much money here. But I am much better,
and want to go to school.
Please tell Auntie Yvonne and all the rest to write to me. I am longing to
hear from them.
I am Red Riding Hood in the pantomime. The rehearsal is at 10 o'clock.
It is rather foggy this morning and we have had frost a few times last
week.
Give everyone my love.
How is Quarry River these days, and how are you all?
Lots of love
Celia

27th December 1959
Dear Mummy and Daddy,
Thanks very much for the cake and postal orders.

I have eaten all the cake already, but I haven't spent the postal orders.
Its is quite cold here today but the sun shone this morning and Stephanie and I and some others went for a long walk in the grounds.
Tell Auntie Doonie thanks very much for her postal orders and give me her address in your next letter.
Give Auntie Babs and Uncle Burton my love and thank them for their card and handkerchief.
Lots of love,
Celia

18ᵗʰ January 1960
Dear Mummy and Daddy,
Thank you very much for the lovely book you sent me. On my birthday, all the patients gave me a lovely fruitcake with pink and red roses on it.
The other night, some of us from Wantage went to a film called 'She Didn't Say No' in the hall of the main building. It was for adults, but Nurse Lannon said I could go. It was very nice and I enjoyed it very much. When we were coming home from it, some OT girls came with us and there were some boys which we didn't see hidden behind some trees, and when we were passing there, some of the OT girls said, 'Come on girls' and as soon as they said it, the boys said, 'Come on boys' and pelted them down with snow balls.
There is a film coming here on Thursday or Friday called 'The Bells of St Mary's'. I hear that it is nice, so I'm going to see it with the rest.
Lots of love
Celia

27ᵗʰ February 1960
Dear Mummy,
The sun is shining today, and I've just had my pills. I am managing alright. I hope to be going for a walk today. Every Thursday I go to 'Physical Training'. It is quite fun and I meet lots of other girls.
I am wondering when I am going to school and what is going to happen to me.
I hope everybody is well at home. There is not much news to write here. I haven't seen auntie Hélène for a long time, and I think she is lovely.
I hope Rosie does well in class and Claudie. Please write soon. Give my love to everyone.
Lots of love, Celia

Paradise Plums and Cocoa Beans:
Schizophrenia and Celia's Longing for Home

3 April 1960
Dear Daddy,
I am still in "the bin", with all the others who've been chucked out.
For breakfast today we had: Fried bread and bacon, toast and butter,
porridge and tea. But instead of tea I had milk and instead of porridge I
had cornflakes and milk and sugar. So you see what I mean when I say I
want fruit and 'topie tabs', because the food is ghastly. So please send
some more grapefruit and anything that will keep before the crop is over.
Please hurry up and send me to school in England and please take me out
for the summer holidays. Because I would like to go to school in England
or if you would rather take me out for good back to "Trin".
Your loving daughter, Celia
P.S. Write soon

8 April 1960
Dear Mummy,
I got your letter today and I got the crate of grapefruit yesterday. I went
swimming yesterday with 'Paulette' the French maid and it was good fun
especially trying to dive, I dived from the second highest board, which I
thought was good.
I am now a recruit for rangers and I am longing to be one of them, right
now I am knitting squares for them. I am longing to get out of here and I
am wondering when I will but it is all up to you. The doctors never tell me
if I am getting out so would you please write and tell them that you're
going to send me to school because there is nothing wrong with me now,
at least not in my opinion.
We are having for lunch, 1st course: Tomato soup; 2nd course: Fish and
chips; 3rd course: Apple and bread and butter pudding with custard, and
the chef is off for two weeks leave so you can imagine what the food is
like. Especially the custard it has no eggs or anything.
I went for a couple of walks in the grounds today, which is what I do every
day, because there is nothing else to do.
The sister here and the nurses are a bit strict but never mind, if only there
were no grown ups in the world.
I am getting a lot of new dresses and skirts and two pairs of shoes because
I am desperately in need.
Everybody liked the pictures you sent so thanks very much for them.
I am sorry that there is no more news. Give my love to everyone.
Lots of love, Celia

12 April 1960
Dear Mummy,
Thank you very much for your letter.
There is not much news except that the weather is rather gloomy and the croquet is up on the lawn.
Everybody thought 'Andy' looked very nice in the photos as I showed them to quite a few people they also thought 'Claudia' and 'you' looked nice.
I walked round the 'golf course' quite a few times yesterday but as soon as I had walked about half way round it would start to rain so I had to rush back to Wantage.
Has Auntie Yvonne gone to Puerto Rico yet? I forgot the date that she told me she was going.
How are Pauline and Bernard?
I am very glad about the weddings. Give both couples my love.
I am desperately in need of clothes, but 'Sister Yates' says that she is going to get me some 'frocks' and one pair of 'Plimsolls' and a pair of ordinary shoes because mine are worn out. Would you please send me a manicure set as I haven't got one!
Have the 'Fortiers' been up to Auntie Yvonne's lately? If you see them please give them all my love, and ask 'Viviane' to write me if she feels like it, and I should be pleased to hear from anyone. As I like getting letters from home with all the news.
With Love
From Celia
P.S. Please give my love to Daddy and the children including Paul if he is there.

15ᵗʰ April 1960
Dear Paul,
I haven't heard from you for ages, please hurry and write.
Life here is much the same as usual, 'Dr Tennant' 'the boo' is making the rounds as usual on Sunday morning at around ten o'clock, he is very nice really, and I like him very much, but he is quite old, wears glasses, is very tall, and has stooped shoulders, eyes like a hawk, and plays golf every Sunday morning.
There is another doctor called Doctor MacLaughlin who I try to dodge every day, there is another doctor who is very nice, and I never dodge, sometimes I dodge Dr Tennant, when my pal Stephi is here, he makes her feel bad.

Yesterday I went for a few walks round the golf course, it was quite interesting, and there is a little shack down in the woods at the bottom of a track which is out of bounds, one day when me and Stephi went there, there was a dead rat and dead bird on the stones, which form the doorway, but they are gone now.

At the moment I am knitting squares, for the refugees, as I am a recruit for rangers.

Give my love to everyone at home.

Lots of love, Celia

16th April 1960

Dear Daddy,

I am starving for fruit, so would you please send me as much as you can, of any fruit that would keep and some 'tambrans' and 'portugals' and 'King Oranges' and bananas but not too many tambrans because I don't know if English people like them as Stephanie sampled a tambran ball and immediately gave it back to me.

There are a few fruits here that you can take, such as 'Dr Tennant's' pears and apples in the orchard, which he leaves there to rot, but they haven't started to bear yet.

Please daddy would [you send] me lots of mangos such as 'Juillet' and 'calabash' and any other kind which would keep.

Lots of Love, Celia

18th April 1960

Dear Mummy,

Please do something for me if you ever loved me. Because Northampton is so damn deadly dull, and so damn deadly boring, that it drives me up the wall, and you can never see the people you love, because of the horrible Irish nurses who say they are looking after you but they are not, for example they took me into town to church, and I nearly fainted, so if you love me take me out of Northampton, because I am deadly sick of it, you have no idea how much I miss you all, please answer my letters if you care the slightest bit for me, and the food gets <u>worse</u> and <u>worse</u> each day, and it is freezing cold and I have no warm clothes, and English people are so damn stuck up and sometimish (sic), and rude I am going to write a letter to Auntie Hélène now.

Your darling and ever loving daughter, Celia.

P.S. Thank you for the Easter Egg

19th April 1960

Dear Rosie,

Thank you for your letter darling, and the card, it certainly cheered me up, everybody always wants to see my photographs and I have to explain them everything and why some of them looked so windy, it was because of Janet, do you remember 'hurricane Janet', and when we all used to sing, Janet I'm begging you hard, Janet not Trinidad, you blow away the whole of Grenada, Barbados, St Kitts and St Lucia.

Janet hide in the mountain, and so on.

Do you remember it? And, 'So much a damn Barbadian in Trinidad?' Do you remember them both? I hope you do.

Please send me all the latest calypsos and Carnival pictures you can get.

Tell me all the latest news, Happy Easter, did you get the Easter cards I sent you yet? I sent one to Pauline and Bernard and the Cadizes and so on. Write and let me know if you have.

Love

Celia

19th April 1960

Dear Raymond,

How are you? I am fine except that they keep on giving us coffee and tea, I had to steal a cup of ovaltine now this morning. I hope you are being good and growing up nicely.

Everybody in England asks about you all, and wants to know your names, including Andrew. This morning I watched a bit of golf then came inside to write to you.

I wish you a very happy Easter, and God bless you darling. Are you all still playing cricket and rounders? I wish I could be there with you all.

Summer is coming so the apples will start to bear and the pears, so I will have to go and raid, like I did last summer.

Give Muffin and the crowd my love and Pauline and Bernard.

Lots of love, Celia.

P.S. Write soon.

21st April 1960

Dear Daddy,

I am damn sorry to say but I am damn vexed with that damn mother of mine, and I hate her and I shall never speak to her again. I wrote to her and explained how fed up I was with this place, and she writes back a set of damned bull-shit. Northampton is damn stale and damn boring and I am fed up and it is Easter now and I would like to have a holiday perhaps at Aunt Hélène's in Surrey, so that I can forget that damn mother of mine, and she won't be able to write me.

Daddy, I am well, I am healthy, I want to go to school. Please do not show this letter to Mummy. I am hungry and I want fruit.

Lots of love, Celia.

P.S. Excuse handwriting, I am in a temper.

25ᵗʰ April 1960

Dear Daddy,

How are you, I am okay except for a horrible nurse here called 'nurse Lannon', she is always lashing me. She also called me 'a cheeky little blighter'? Anyway, I am becoming a ranger, so I would like permission to carry 'jack-knife' or a pen-knife. When I was a guide I had a pen-knife so now I would like a jack-knife.

There is not much news to tell except for the horrible Irish nurses who I don't speak to, but one of them, nurse Lannon, keeps lashing me.

Lots of love, your daughter

Celia

P.S. I have to go to tea now, excuse hand-writing.

P.P.S. Don't forget, fruit and food and a wallet and a scarf.

25ᵗʰ April 1960

Dear Paul,

I am fine except for a cold which was given to me by 'Nurse Lannon' she let me freeze in bed all morning because I didn't want to go to church, she is always lashing me and fighting me, in the bath and calling me 'a cheeky little blighter'.

She is Irish by the way, I wish you were here to protect me.

There is another Irish nurse here called 'Nurse Gaughan' who I don't speak to, I don't speak to 'Nurse Lannon' either, but they both 'howl for my blood' all day and harass me.

Anyway if they do it again, dey go see.

Life here is dreadfully dull, and boring. But I can imagine you all having a lovely time in the Easter holidays.

Lots of love Celia.

P.S. Give my love to H.P. Gantaume and all the family.

27th April 1960
Dear Daddy,
I am in dire need of fruit please, send some oranges, grapefruit, anything.
Please get me out of here, it is up to you what you are going to do with
me, because I'm sick and tired of Northampton.
Your daughter, Celia.
P.S. This is for you not Mummy. Hoping to hear from you soon. There is a
woman here who is having a baby and she isn't married. She terrifies me.

Undated *1960*
Dear Daddy,
When am I coming home? I was thinking of coming this month, please
come over soon and take me back, it costs 15 guineas a week to stay here
and at home it is much cheaper. Kitty Udenburg is my teacher and look
where I am.
Love Celia.

Undated *1960*
Dear Pablo [brother Paul],
I went swimming on Saturday with Manolo a Spanish boy and 'Dulcie
Boone' and Miss 'Verdon' alias 'Vernie' and a few others, we had a lot of
fun.
I wrote to 'Rosie' Rosalind Fernandes the other day, I hope she answers
my letter soon.
Les Petites Soldats Adios, Celia Marguerite Anne-Marie de Verteuil.
P.S. Prince Charles would like to hear from you very much, remember we
are their first cousins.

Undated *1960*
Dear Paul,
I am missing you and Raymond terribly, give the lord abbot my love. I
hope the plan [?] works out and give Robert my love. I am coming home
soon. Please give Michael Rostant my love and Brother Bernard.
I hope this letter gets to you.
Lots of love, Celia Marguerite Anne-Marie de Verteuil

This collection of letters from Celia include other members of the family
and while commenting on her life in "damn stale and damn boring
Northampton", her previous life in Trinidad is very much in the

foreground. She still uses Trinidadian slang: her, "if they do it again, <u>dey go see</u>", immediately followed by, "life here is so dreadfully dull and boring", but she can still imagine everyone at home, "having a lovely time in the Easter holidays". Her longing for some tropical fruit is enduring and almost Proustian in what it conjures up for her.

Celia's letters were often sent to us in fits and starts. Sometimes we received two or three a week, followed by a gap of several weeks. This may be accounted for by a more acute phase in her condition. During the month of October 1960, Celia's doctor and the Chief Superintendent at St Andrew's Hospital had written to our parents that, "recently there has been some Improvement in Celia's condition, following a further course of electroplexy and we hope that she may soon be fit to leave hospital". Dad's immediate reply to him included the following, "As you are aware, my wife has suffered two severe nervous breakdowns, as a result of Celia's prolonged mental illness, and she has only just recovered from the last bout". (It seemed at times that Dad was indeed choosing between his daughter and his wife). "Furthermore, there are five young children to consider. Consequently, it is with a great deal of caution that we view Celia's immediate return to Trinidad."

Dad's conflicted emotional state can again be found in his letter to Aunt Hélène: "If the cause of the present phase of her illness is due to lack of parental affection or home life as the doctor seems to suggest then we shall have no option but to take steps to bring her back immediately! – and hope for the best."

At this point, a year after leaving Trinidad, Celia's return home was being contemplated, but it was never going to be simple. In November of 1960, alarm bells rang. A letter sent to Dr Michael Beaubrun was the reason for this.

Postmarked 18th August 1960, and addressed to Dr Evelyn Beaubrun it read:

Dear Evelyn,
I have discovered the ruins of 'Porto Bello', I think that is what you asked for, if not, tell Daddy.
I have recognised Moscow spies, if you don't want the information give it to 'daddy'.
Love
Celia de Verteuil

As a result of this letter from Celia, Dad wrote that, "Dr Beaubrun is strongly of the opinion that Celia still requires 'institutional care and could not be treated as an out-patient at the moment'." (11th November 1960)

Mum wrote to Aunt Hélène with similar concerns. Referring to a letter from Dr Tennant, she writes, "He has come back to the old question that the Oxford Regional Board probably won't continue to pay for her [Celia] and that in his opinion, Celia should leave the hospital." (14th November 1960)

The old questions of financial support for Celia in England, and the possibility of her return to Trinidad, continued to rumble. Further on, in the same letter, Mum continues, "We can't understand the change in Celia, because her letters had shown a steady improvement up to April [1960] when she stopped writing to me altogether, although I wrote to her every week. From then on she has written only to Esmé and to other members of the family and there has been a steady deterioration both as to subject matter and to handwriting."

Celia as a toddler in Trinidad (1947)

Celia in fancy dress as Mrs Micawber, aged four

Celia, second right with Mummy and siblings: Andrew and Geoffrey not yet born (1955)

Celia and brother Paul age 7 or 8

Celia, sitting, first left holding me on her lap. Assorted siblings and cousins (1954)

DESCRIPTION - SIGNALEMENT

	Bearer—Titulaire	Wife—Femme
Profession		
Place and date of birth Lieu et date de naissance	TRINIDAD T.W.T 13TH JANUARY 1945	
Residence Résidence	TRINIDAD T.W.T	
Height Taille	5 ft 1 in.	ft. in.
Colour of eyes Couleur des yeux	HAZEL	
Colour of hair Couleur des cheveux	BROWN	
Special peculiarities Signes particuliers		

CHILDREN — ENFANTS

Name-Nom	Date of birth-Date de naissance	Sex-Sexe

Usual Signature of Bearer
Signature du Titulaire

Usual Signature of Wife
Signature de sa Femme

Bearer
(Titulaire)

Wife
(Femme)

(Photo)

Passport photo, aged 14 (1959)

Celia and Peter (1982)

DESCRIPTION

	BEARER	WIFE
Name:	CELIA MARGUERITE ANN MARIE DE VERTEUIL	
Profession:		
Date of Birth:	13 JANUARY 1945	
Place of Birth:	TRINIDAD	
Place of Residence:	ENGLAND	
Registration Number:	—	
Height:	162 cm	cm
Colour of Eyes:	HAZEL	
Colour of Hair:	BLACK	

CHILDREN

Name	Date of Birth	Sex
....	....	....
....	....	....

PHOTOGRAPH OF BEARER   PHOTOGRAPH OF WIFE

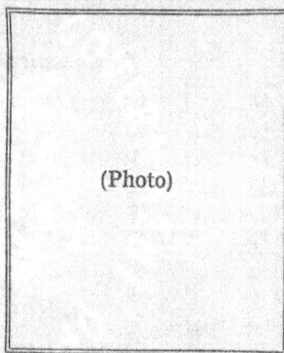

(Photo)

Celia de Verteuil

Signature   Signature

Passport photo, aged 38 (1983)

Celia in late middle age

Celia and me in Northampton (1998)

Celia (centre) with Rosie on the left and me on the right.
Northampton (2005)

Staying connected – Visiting, 1972-2012

Apart from one letter dated 1962, there is a lengthy gap before the surviving correspondence resumes in the late 1970s, when Celia was in her mid-30s and still at St Andrew's. As before, the theme of a return to home and family in Trinidad is dominant. The following letter shows the request for a return in a different way, as if hoping for a different result.

24th December 1978
St Andrew's Hospital
Northampton.
Dear Mum and Dad,
Thank you for your beautiful letter. It was a pleasure receiving it. I am happy and very well. Maybe I did not explain myself properly. I did not mean I want to come home to live. What I meant is that, I would like to have a holiday in Trinidad, 3-4 weeks if that is okay with you all. I am longing to see each and every one of you and so I think a holiday will be the best thing for me. It will be nice to have a break from St Andrew's. Please think it over carefully and let Dr Eames know as soon as possible. All my love to each and everyone of you.
Your loving daughter, Celia.

The 1970s was also the time that I began to visit Celia when I came to live in England. In the year of my marriage to Peter, 1979, his parents, Margery and John Holliday, were living temporarily in Trinidad and were thus able to meet all of my family there. In July and August of that year, my parents visited us in London and Peter and I made the trip to Northampton with them. Mum had not seen Celia for twenty years and it was the last time that Celia and I were to see our mother, since she already had the aggressive lymphoma which was to end her life two years later. Her letter to Dr Tennant in October 1979 on her return to Trinidad shows what was on her mind at the time. She was asking what level of information she should be giving Celia about her illness, and whether this should be the "whole truth", which was what she was preparing to tell me and my other siblings.

The importance of those letters at the time in helping Celia to feel connected with us and another reality has already been stated. There is more to say about their role in her identity preservation and management, by providing a continuity of memories, contacts, and hopes of returning to her family in Trinidad; the letters functioned as a kind of passport, a means of identification with somewhere else. Through this correspondence, she constructed and preserved her sense of self and 'managed' the stigma associated with her schizophrenia.

To help us understand something of this process, I refer to Erving Goffman, whose classic study *Stigma* (1963) draws our attention to 'identity ambivalence' among stigmatised individuals such as mental patients. Here, information management is seen as central to personal identity. Being socially and psychologically identified with the other patients but also repelled and ashamed of stereotypical behaviour and the acting-out of negative attributes imputed to them by members of that group. It is a double bind, with attempts to 'normify' behaviour and 'clean up' the conduct of others in the group.

Institutionalisation had left its imprint on Celia and she could not always 'normify' her conduct. Her habit of collecting and storing cigarette butts in her handbag and her eating and drinking habits were not always 'cleaned up'. To me, this was uncomfortable as it seemed to display a regression to an earlier, more child-like, state, for example the way she sucked repeatedly from her drinks. Her ambivalent identity could be seen most acutely in her 'distancing' of other patients present where they displayed any undesirable behaviour of her own kind, while being with us 'normals'. For example, she would apologise if another patient walked by inappropriately dressed.

Clare Allan has written on mental health issues for the UK newspaper the *Guardian*. She wrote of her own admission to a mental hospital approximately fifteen years ago, of how her freedom was replaced with life on a mixed ward, with fellow residents behaving alarmingly, and an extreme lack of privacy.

Ken Kesey's *One Flew Over The Cuckoo's Nest* resonates and, generally, it is not rare to find accounts, in both literature and journalism, even when contexts of time and place are very different. Celia's letters, and our interactions with her, helped her to 'pass' into our reality and to preserve her sense of self.

Another aspect at work here is what Erving Goffman describes as 'sheltering'. This can occur in regard to whole categories of the stigmatised. He cites as an example neighbourhoods close to hospitals where patients are receiving skin grafting treatment; how local people develop a capacity to interact 'normally' with such people.

Here, I am reminded of the small grocery which serviced Celia's immediate neighbourhood; a place of very high tolerance for psychotic behaviour. She would also have experienced in the same neighbourhood a polar opposite response: prejudice and hostility. The point is, she would have been aware and had to 'manage' these 'adaptations'; hers and others', both inside and outside the hospital environment. It would have been a part of her social identity and defined her as someone with schizophrenia.

While so much of the daily life in the hospital was communal, Celia showed that she could achieve and maintain some control over her life as well as adhering to a basic ward ethos and routine. She could 'work the system' and at times subvert it. Needing some support in the area of personal hygiene and grooming, Celia enjoyed dressing up, wearing make-up and jewellery, particularly a gold medal that belonged to Mum; all items which expressed and presented her individuality. Without a doubt, her personal signifier was her handbag. Much more than an accessory, it contained the unique combination of her life history. A feature of her life as a mental patient was that she owned nothing. Her handbag was the only object personal to her, which she, quite literally, could hold on to. It was invested with a rare permanence which even her clothes lacked as there was no guarantee that they would still be hers when (and if) they were returned from the hospital's laundry. As a repository of the contents of her life past and present: her letters, lipstick and her cigarettes, which were far more more than just objects in themselves. Their function was to allow for a sense of identity. For example, in providing a way into memories and contacts, her letters from family and friends allowed her to pass into another reality 'outside' (of the institution). Her lipstick signified gender and the personal grooming required for her self-presentation. Her numerous packets of cigarettes functioned as 'currency' on the wards. This signified an informal network of alliances, friendships and benefits; a system organised by the patients, running in parallel with the official dispensing of cigarettes on a controlled basis by the staff to the patients. What is instructive about this is how these adjustments and ways of 'working the system' confirmed Celia's status as a mental patient.

By subverting the effects of institutional life through a myriad of small acts, Celia, like so many in long-term institutional care, was able to preserve her identity and, at times, challenge the labels ascribed to her kind, by the society at large. The tenacity, through which Celia remained 'engaged' at so many levels and over so many years of institutional life, is an important statement for being socially connected. This applies equally to many different groups in our society - for example the elderly, who, for various reasons, risk becoming 'invisible' and disconnected from the mainstream.

What is the perspective of the family or carer of someone with schizophrenia or serious mental illness? For this group, what is the reality of engagement with their sick relative?

For our family, this experience was defined by Celia's absence from the home. I have therefore provided an account of a time when, typically, families come together, under the heading 'Christmas is a sad time'. Having Celia in our family defined us all and meant that we too were subject to 'identity ambivalence' such as our parents' adoption of 'protective' strategies to keep the truth of Celia's schizophrenia from us. I am still uncertain as to whether or not they fully understood the nature of her schizophrenia, or really wanted to. What it points to is our awareness of stigma, of what others knew or did not know, and who needed to be told about Celia.

After so many years, I still find talking about Celia and her mental illness problematic. A friend who has known me for almost 40 years said to me quite recently that she always knew from what was unsaid, as much as from the little that I told her about Celia, of the importance of my sister in my life.

In a sense, Celia 'inhabited' us; this is ironic, given her physical absence from our lives. Equally significant was the fact that she continued to care about and love us to the end of her days. She was 'unsheltered' by us and we were 'unencumbered' by her presence. These are some of the paradoxes that have transpired on reflection and in the re-writing of her story and ours.

Christmas is a Sad Time

The annual shopping round for Christmas presents for Celia was an important ritual for my mother and later inherited by me. Gift-giving is the glue which helps to bind us together but, as with all human interactions, both the occasion and the giving are not without their complications. Questions needing to be answered – what to buy? In Celia's case, the question of what she needed or wanted, or her present clothes size, for example, had to be imagined. I always felt great anxiety about Christmas shopping for Celia and would end up with a bag of small things that she would have to open on Christmas Day. By wrapping each present in different coloured/patterned paper, and labelling them from different members of the family, I was able (I thought) to maintain a more authentic family feel to her Christmas. Often siblings would send presents and cards but when they did not, I 'proxied' for them, by providing a gift on their behalf.

What really mattered at Christmas time was the cake for Celia and one of my earliest memories is of the cake-making in our kitchen at home in Arima. Holding on to the legs of the kitchen bar stools, I was still too young to climb up and sit at the same level as the bowl and my mother's arm, which stirred the wonderful mixture. Arm, bowl and the wooden beater joined together as one, intent on the job in hand.

The build-up to this day was the sight and smell of dried fruit soaking in rum in large glass jars, for several months beforehand. On the appointed day, my siblings and I would hover around the kitchen, awaiting the prize at the end: the large mixing bowl and the wooden spoon, which we had to share like a litter of puppies. We licked and lapped until both were clean of cake mixture and the evidence all around our mouths.

Once cooked and cooled, the cake would be iced, providing more treats, but the pure sweetness of the cake icing could not match the fruit mixture, with its intoxicating smell, taste and effects of rum. Maybe it was Old Oak, the finest quality Trinidad rum. Celia's cake, when ready, would be packed and parcelled for overseas posting. Parcels had to go well in advance - which, I suppose, still applies today – at that time of year because of the pressure on the postal service.

Mum made my wedding cake (a three-tier job) in what must have been the same way and I received it in the post, ready for my London wedding.

What that cake conjured up was far greater than the sum of its parts.

To return to Celia's cake, it was a happy association with Celia and my formative experience of Mum in the kitchen at that time, but it could also be a sad time because of what and who the cake reminded us of.

For me, Christmas is a sad time. The requirement to celebrate and have fun as a family did not then, and does not now, sit comfortably with the feelings of loss and the pain of Celia's absence. These are feelings which grew in intensity with age and although I have tried many ways of 'doing' Christmas, the sadness remains and it has not been unusual for me to be in tears on Christmas Day. This resonates with my sister Rosie's comment that Mum was always sad at Christmas, when "we were together and Celia was not there."

Long after Mum's death, whether or not I made Celia's Christmas cake or gave her a commercial version, it continued to be an important item on the list. There is a symmetry in the fact that Celia often talked about making a ginger cake, rich in fruit, with a staff member. As it happens, I made a bread pudding for us to share after Celia's funeral in 2012. It too was rich in dried fruit that I had soaked in rum – Old Oak, given to me as a 'duty free gift' on arrival at the airport by a visiting relative from Trinidad. A potent symbol, a cake, which allowed us to celebrate and to remember. It was far more than just a cake!

Afterthoughts – What is Schizophrenia?

Psychos on the streets

Care in Crisis as mental patients are freed to kill

The popular press often run with such headlines, highlighting their role in 'protecting the public' from the threat of a dangerous form of madness. Everyday speech contains many stigmatising and dehumanising words to refer to the mentally ill. Examples include: *lunatic, barking mad, schizo, fruitcake*. Few of us have any direct experience of a mental disorder so it is not difficult to gain the wrong impression.

At the other extreme, we may of course enhance the status of known individuals through their madness. The idea of the 'mad genius' is prevalent in art history, writing about music and literary criticism. Vincent van Gogh and Virginia Woolf have both been characterised in this way. The vast majority of sufferers are in fact neither dangerous nor creative geniuses. What is not in dispute is that many will indeed appear irrational and behave in ways that are difficult for us to understand. But understand we must, if we are to develop effective treatments for the severely mentally ill, as in typical forms of schizophrenia.

Schizophrenia exists in all countries and cultures, across all classes, income groups and genders. It is more persistent than we may think and we have a duty of care to the, roughly, one person in a hundred among us who may experience this disorder at some time in their lives. This lifetime risk of 1% is about the same as that for developing rheumatoid arthritis (See C. Frith and E. Johnstone, *A Very Short Introduction to Schizophrenia*, 2003, OUP:p1).

Trying to map the territory of schizophrenia is not an easy task so for this I have relied on the OUP series as a guide. My plan follows the headings and takes the form of an approximation of the text:

- The historical context for understanding the symptoms of schizophrenia
- Areas of uncertainty and weakness
- Genetic, psycho-social and biological

The experience of schizophrenia (a) Psychological and Social Considerations and (b) The Hearing of Voices.

It may be possible, by reading first-hand accounts, to understand what it is like to experience this form of madness. Frith and Johnstone provide a particularly memorable account quoted by Sir Aubrey Lewis in 1967, written by an eighteen-year-old boy who had been ill for at least a year.

"I am more and more losing contact with my environment and with myself. Instead of taking an interest in what goes on and caring about what happens with my illness, I am all the time losing my emotional contact with everything including myself. What remains is only an abstract knowledge of what goes on around me and of the internal happenings in myself..."

(Christopher Frith and Eve Johnstone, *Schizophrenia: A Very Short Introduction*, 2003:p2, by permission of Oxford University Press)

This account concerns the so-called 'negative' aspects of schizophrenia, seen clearly in the gradual withdrawal from the world and the emotional disconnection, where "what remains is only an abstract knowledge".

The account continues somewhat tragically:

"I cannot picture anything more frightful than for a well-endowed cultivated human being to live through his own gradual deterioration fully aware of it all the time. But that is what is happening to me."

Here we can identify 'negative' symptoms as a 'loss' of function as opposed to 'positive' symptoms, which could be said to 'add' another dimension. The account by John Percival (1938), the son of the British Prime Minister Spencer Percival, whose experience of madness had many of the 'positive' aspects, is as follows:

"Only a short time before I was confined to my bed I began to hear voices, at first only close to my ear, afterwards in my head, or as if one was whispering in my ear, - or in various parts of the room. These voices I obeyed or endeavoured to obey, and believed almost implicitly... These voices commanded me to do, and make me believe a number of false and terrible things."

(Christopher Frith and Eve Johnstone, *Schizophrenia: A Very Short Introduction*, 2003, OUP:p6, by permission of Oxford University Press)

Frith and Johnstone tell us that John was kept in asylums for about three years, but he gradually recovered and began writing about his illness a year or so later. John's recovery has left us a rare first-person account of the experience of schizophrenia, as it would have been unlikely that such an account could have been written when he was very ill.

Celia never used the term 'schizophrenia' or indeed 'mental illness' with reference to herself. Clearly, she did traverse the parallel worlds of the so-called sane and insane. Her identifications with either one or other were strong or weak at different times. I recall one of her psychiatrists at St Andrew's Hospital questioning her diagnosis of schizophrenia. For much of the time, what Celia presented to me were the effects of her years of institutional life.

That Celia was unable to vocalise her experience of her schizophrenia does not mean that she was unaware of living in parallel worlds. I was sometimes aware that she might have been hearing voices when our communication broke down and her thoughts became disconnected. Her facial expression and body language could be hostile and agitated or relaxed and jokey at that moment. I suppose this depended on the nature of the interference she was experiencing. It is not uncommon for a person with schizophrenia to refer to their voices and in a social context for the voice to be invited into the exchange. For this to be socially acceptable, there must be an open and shared recognition that fixed identities do not apply but rather a plurality of existence.

In addition to the previously mentioned auditory interventions, which varied in length and were not always evident on our visits to Celia, were the persecutory and false beliefs. That is, they were false to us. On a literal reading of them they did not correspond to reality as understood by us. To Celia, however, they were far from false and must have reflected hugely how she felt about and understood her life. That 'someone was out to get her' was often accompanied by her feeling threatened by my asking her too many questions. She would refer to herself as 'Great Britain's slave' and say that she was adopted or had two children. At other times, she would say she worked on a farm. What does this tell us? It is that her psychotic voice was personal to her. The imagery, idiosyncratic in form, a reflection of herself with the power perhaps to process her psychosis. Perhaps evacuating what was in her mind and transferring it in some way. Where this was happening, the mismatch between the personal and social meanings in her thought and speech meant that conversation in any taken-for-granted sense was difficult. However, Celia was able to take control and, in that sense, be accountable for some forms of exchange, often in the form of sequencing daily events - past and future - which could be talked about with us. They were repeatable topics and strategies that supported such exchanges and trust between us.

The Historical Context for Understanding Collections of

Symptoms

Both the 'positive' and the 'negative' symptoms characteristic of a diagnosis of schizophrenia originated in the nineteenth century. Between 1893 and 1927, Emil Kraepelin defined his ideas on mental disorders. In *Lehrbuch der Psychiatrie* (*Textbook of Psychiatry*), he created a classification system and clarified his diagnostic ideas. He divided the broad class of functional psychosis into two, essentially on the basis of outcome. The first category, which he called 'manic depressive insanity', pursued a fluctuating course with frequent relapses, but with full recovery between episodes. The second he termed 'dementia praecox'. He believed that the cluster of symptoms and signs that had the characteristic course and outcome of dementia praecox had a specific pathology in the brain and a specific cause, though essentially nothing was known of either the pathology or the cause during his lifetime. The symptoms that he emphasised included auditory and tactile hallucinations, delusions, incoherent speech, blunted emotions, negativity and lack of insight. Nevertheless, he appreciated that the condition was diverse and difficult to classify. He wrote:

"There is certainly a whole series of phases which frequently return but between them are such numerous transitions that, in spite of all efforts, it appears impossible at present to delimit them sharply and to assign each case without objection to a different form."

(Christopher Frith and Eve Johnstone, *Schizophrenia: A Very Short Introduction*, 2003:p30, by permission of Oxford University Press)

Another early pioneer in the field was Eugen Bleuler (1857-1939), who coined the term 'schizophrenia'. He was influenced by the ideas being developed by Freud and saw schizophrenia in terms very different to the neuro-pathological ones envisaged by Kraepelin. His term meant 'split mind' and was intended to describe a loosening of the associations between the different functions of the mind so that thoughts became disconnected and coordination between emotional, cognitive and volitional processes became weaker. He considered that ambivalence (the presence of conflicting emotions and desires), autism (lack of social contact), lack of volition (loss of will), and abnormal affectivity (bizarre or blunted emotional responses) were fundamental features that could be observed in every case while the hallucinations, catatonic features, delusions and other elements of behavioural disturbance emphasised by Kraepelin were secondary phenomena which might or might not be present. Bleuler's ideas became influential in the USA but in Europe, Kraepelin's concept of dementia praecox, although that term was replaced by 'schizophrenia', continued to dominate diagnostic habits. As a result, different diagnostic habits developed on the two sides of the Atlantic.

Whether we are comparing one patient with another or the same patient at different times, the signs and symptoms of schizophrenia vary markedly. The presence of, for example, hallucinations, does not necessarily indicate the presence in the patient of poverty of speech or disorganised behaviour. For each individual patient, and at different phases of their illness, there might be varying combinations of symptoms. Where to draw the line remains a difficult question as the boundary between normality and psychosis is not clear-cut.

"In practice, most people with a diagnosis of schizophrenia have a severe and enduring mental disorder that will persist or recur despite treatment. These people have obvious and persistent delusions and hallucinations, and are no longer in touch with reality. The diagnostic line has been drawn here on the basis that such people will not be able to function in our society without considerable help."

(Christopher Frith and Eve Johnstone, *Schizophrenia: A Very Short Introduction*, 2003, OUP:pP44-46, by permission of Oxford Univeristy Press)

Standardised diagnostic procedure, as for example, the DSM (Diagnostic and Statistical Manual of Mental Disorder) – IV criteria for schizotypal personality disorder for a diagnosis act as guidelines but of course do not eliminate the need for skilled and experienced clinicians.

Areas of Uncertainty and Weakness

People with schizophrenia are not mentally disabled and do not suffer a physical abnormality in the brain, yet the standard treatment is using drugs. There is a basic flaw in putting the collection of signs and symptoms associated with schizophrenia within a neuro-pathological framework.

While recognising the value of 'antipsychotics' in treating delusions and hallucinations and their efficacy when used as maintenance treatment in preventing relapse, the evidence concerns positive symptoms only. This relates to the capacity of certain drugs to create or suppress psychotic hallucinations and delusions and this capacity is taken as clear evidence that these experiences can be caused by changes in brain function. Specifically, with schizoid-typical conditions, the clinical efficacy of antipsychotics is that they block or inhibit dopamine transmission in the brain. The nature of these changes and the clues and markers relating to the negative or deficit symptoms remain a mystery. This is regrettable since these can be some of the more debilitating effects of schizophrenia. This requires a different model of understanding and approach to treatment and highlights the opposition between the organic/biological and the psycho-social model of madness. The professional expression of this difference is in the practices of psychiatrists, as compared to psycho-analysts. The words of a psycho-analyst in conversation with Barbara Taylor is telling in this respect:

"The difference between ourselves and organically based psychiatrists, is that they <u>know</u> what is going on. We haven't the faintest idea, so we have to listen to our patients."

(Barbara Taylor, *The Last Asylum*, 2014:p88, Copyright © Barbara Taylor, 2014)

Psychiatrists can be credited with knowing about brain chemistry and the effects of medication on the brain. In comparison, for the psycho-analyst, it is the relationship between therapist and patient that is in focus during treatment. In this context, listening to the patient refers quite specifically to being a 'mind' for the other. This may be understood as a sort of mental space which allows the patient to both act out and project their psychosis and at the same time be helped to understand their reality and find meaning through it. Whichever models are adopted in treatment, the impact on sufferers ultimately affects outcomes and recovery states.

Biological, Genetic and Psycho-Social Aspects

There is evidence to suggest a predisposition within some families towards mental illness. For example, studies of children who have a schizophrenic biological parent but who were adopted at birth have found that they are at greater risk of developing schizophrenia, but not if there was schizophrenia only among their adoptive relatives.

Does it matter whether schizophrenia in families is due to shared environment or to shared genetic material? In my view, they could both play a role in the development of schizophrenia or any other form of mental illness and both offer important clues to what might contribute to the cause of the condition.

Precise bio-chemical markers remain unknown while there is some indication that schizophrenia is a neuro-developmental condition in which the basic abnormality arises very early in life, possibly in the foetus or around the time of birth. As a result of some kind of compensation, the abnormality does not lead to symptoms until early adult life.

Frith and Johnstone remark that "we do not know how this compensation might be achieved or why it finally breaks down".

(Christopher Frith and Eve Johnstone, *Schizophrenia: A Very Short Introduction*, 2003, OUP:p104, by permission of Oxford Univeristy Press)

However, the jury remains out on whether these abnormalities are specific to schizophrenia, or how they relate to the various signs and symptoms of the disorder. How can we be certain in following this line of research whether or not an abnormality exists prior to a schizophrenic episode or as a result of care?

(a) Psychological and Social Considerations

The interpretation of just how and why social and psychological factors relate to the causes and treatment of schizophrenia rests on assumptions about the formation of individual personality and selfhood. Events surrounding an individual's life from early infancy are seen as crucial and might include emotional stress factors and trauma as well as patterns of communication and relating within families. These considerations go back to Freud and other psychoanalysts. Freud himself was primarily interested in neuroses rather than psychotic disorders. The application of psychodynamic theories to psychotic people was left to his followers.

Carl Jung worked psycho-therapeutically with schizophrenics and, like Freud, he recognised the power of the unconscious, the disintegration of thought, and the impact of psychosis on 'emotional or affective states' and the disturbing aspects remaining after an episode. Crucial to the understanding and treatment in each individual case is the relationship between the therapist and the patient. Within a psychoanalytic and psychodynamic context, delusions and illusions are seen as an attempt to 'evacuate' as well as a means of 'psychotic' understanding and transformation.

For those working within these traditions, the function of the ego in holding together our internal and external reality seems to fragment and lead to psychosis. That is, the ego cannot process the 'affect' associated with a moment of great emotion, including what might colloquially be termed emotional triggers of stressful life events. It splits off, dissociating from the self, resulting in the loss of unity of personality. This ties in with the examples provided in Frith and Johnstone of patients who attribute the causes of their own action and thoughts to an external agent. In schizophrenia, we are told, something seems to have gone wrong with patients' ability to attribute their actions to themselves.

(b) The Hearing of Voices

In people with schizophrenia there is a mismatch between personal and social meanings. The ability to imagine our thought before having it, or action before performing it, enables us to rapidly check that we are thinking and acting correctly, so that we are not at all surprised when these predicted consequences occur. It is a 'reality check', over which we have control. But what if another 'mind' is telling us what to think and do? The 'voices' that are heard by people with schizophrenia are experienced in this manner.

The most important feature of reality is that it is the same for all of us. If there is a real world out there, it remains roughly the same, whoever is looking at it. The best way of checking the reality of our perceptions is to confirm that they correspond with the experiences of everyone else. This mutual checking applies to not only what we experience with our senses but also those things we believe about the world that are not based directly on our senses. What makes our view of reality 'true' or 'false' is that it is shared for all practical purposes. One of the problems for people with schizophrenia is that their perceptions are no longer appropriately constrained by the perceptions and beliefs of others.

The standardised diagnostic procedure used by psychiatrists is the DSM.But, as with all tools, misused and in the wrong hands, it can lead to misdiagnosis and experience falsely labelled as insane. A further caveat is that what is considered 'normal' and 'abnormal' has historical, social and cultural grounding which is always shifting.

It is to a 'theory of mind' that we look for a relevant account of the class of symptoms in which patients falsely believe that they are being influenced in various ways by other minds – the false beliefs that others are reading your mind (I am reminded here of Celia's reference to 'spies'), that others are persecuting you (paranoid delusions). In all these cases patients 'hallucinate' a non-existent mind that interacts with them. So where do these minds come from? One way of answering the question would be through the notion of 'intentionality'. That is, how we identify the other (mind) as independent from the self, through our ability to read correctly (for all practical purposes) the intentions of others. This is not the same as seeing intentions when none are there. The experience of being able to control our own actions and thoughts is intimately related to our ability to read the intentions of others. But consider, without ownership of thought and action (as in someone telling you what to think and how to act), in what sense are you in control or responsible?

This problem of identification has been discussed by John Campbell: "A patient who supposes that someone else has inserted thoughts into his mind is right about which thoughts they are but wrong about whose thoughts they are." (Christopher Frith and Eve Johnstone, *Schizophrenia: A Very Short Introduction*, 2003, p150, by permission of Oxford University Press)

Along with questions of intentionality, ownership and agency, control and responsibility, must be added the question of personal identity. Much that has been written here and elsewhere about schizophrenia has emphasised its biological (including genetic) nature. There is a weight of convincing data to show that the severity of the positive symptoms of the disorder, the hallucinations and delusions, for example, can be increased or decreased by treatment with drugs. On this bio-medical view, we have to accept that mental qualities such as will and belief are the product of processes in the brain.

One assumption that follows from this is that physical illnesses respond to physical treatments (like drugs) while mental illnesses respond to psychological treatments. It follows that, if a major mental illness like schizophrenia (as claimed) has a physical basis, then there is not a place for psychological treatments. The questionable assumption here is that while physical processes can cause changes in the mental domain, mental processes cannot cause changes in the physical domain. This is unconvincing because there is no logical reason why the flaw should not be in both directions. There are certainly no clear markers in the brain to convince us otherwise. Neither are there any clear indicators that schizophrenia is either partly or wholly a physical disorder. For this reason I feel justified in presenting another viewpoint from which to examine and account for the problem of 'connectedness' and 'disconnectedness' from reality. While 'unconscious inferences' made in the brain can be verified and understood by medical science, the unconscious drives and forces which are part of inter-subjective experiences can be accounted for through psychoanalysis. It is from this perspective that I would like to draw some further insight into the failure to 'hold' the self together and construct and maintain an identity as a unitary whole.

The fragmentation of the self in schizoid states, and the disassociation of thoughts and meanings, may have their roots in an earlier, primary struggle; what some psychoanalysts might describe as the struggle for 'psychic' birth.

Barbara Taylor's examination of an essay by the psychoanalyst Donald Winnicott in *The Last Asylum* (p212) is helpful in describing the processes involved. She commends the imaginative way in which Winnicott describes the processes of becoming oneself and of 'separating' from the other, in that first mother-baby relationship (*The Use of an Object and Relating through Identifications,* D.W. Winnicott in *Playing and Reality*, 1982:Pp101-111). In the mother-baby relationship, Winnicott shows how the human capacity for relating begins in an unconscious dialectic between 'destruction and survival'. Taylor's reading of Winnicott's essay is:

"A new-born baby has no concept of self and other. To a new-born's mind, Baby is everything, and Mother is merely part of Baby, under Baby's omnipotent control. But as an infant matures, this begins to change. Babies, as Winnicott repeatedly reminded his readers, are slave-drivers, petty tyrants who greet every frustration with enraged aggression... In 'good enough' mother-baby relationships, Mother survives these imaginary onslaughts (and the biting and scratching that may accompany them) by just riding them out, and going on looking after Baby without retaliating for the aggression. Each episode of destruction/survival is greeted by the subject/Baby with relief and joy." (Barbara Taylor, *The Last Asylum*, 2014:p213, Copyright © Barbara Taylor, 2014)

Winnicott's point is that the mother's value for the baby, and on which it bases its love, is because she has survived the baby's attempts to destroy her and obliterate herself.

That other great child psychoanalyst, Melanie Klein, also considered this in her concept of the 'paranoid-schizoid position', hints of which, she claimed, remained with us into adulthood.

With each episode of destruction/survival, Mother gradually becomes part of external reality. Infantile omnipotence gives way to Baby's recognition of its reliance on a real and separate person 'out there in the world'.

Affection is born, and concern for Mother, whom Baby can now 'use' – that is, relate to – as an intelligent being and, through this, move forward into healthy maturity.

Taylor draws our attention to a cautionary note from Winnicott that this 'vital phase' of psychological growth is the "the most difficult thing in human development." (Barbara Taylor, *The Last Asylum*, 2014:p213, Copyright © Barbara Taylor, 2014)

Where it fails, it might be due to the baby's destructiveness and the mother not being resilient enough to withstand the baby's aggression.

For the reasons so far outlined, severe mental illness and schizophrenia are highly problematic. That so many sufferers are able to achieve and maintain a coherent persona and social adaptation and function is remarkable. Their reality would seem to be essentially isolating, uncertain and frightening. So much more the reason for a sympathetic response to their condition, rather than the hostile stigmatising and treatment often meted out to them.

Conclusion

Schizophrenia emerges at different times for different people but for the most part it strikes younger people, characteristically in their late teens. Before the illness truly manifests itself, there is the 'prodrome' stage when all is clearly not well. It seems to me that the need for early intervention is critical but also fraught with problems. Why is this?

1. Prodromal symptoms often mirror adolescent behaviour. Dad, in one of his letters, mentions Celia's adolescence as an "additional hurdle" for her to overcome. Some parents may be in denial or simply not intervene as a result of taking behaviour to be part of a normal adolescence.

2. Young people may be treated with/prescribed anti-depressants to combat this part of their illness. This certainly reflects Celia's experience early on.

3. Schizophrenia is often confused with bi-polar and the potential for either no diagnosis or misdiagnosis is vast.

4. The stigma associated with being mentally ill can set off a negative reaction. Those with mental illness are *other* – not like 'us'.

5. An early diagnosis and a label of schizophrenia on the one hand or a reluctance to give a diagnosis and label can both impact negatively on sufferers and their carers. (Saks, *The Centre Cannot Hold, a memoir of my schizophrenia,* 2007:p158)

Early intervention of the right sort before the first psychotic episode occurs is fundamentally important. Current theories of schizophrenia seem to be driven by the experience of the human genome and to a view that genetic disposition leads to the disease. From where I stand, an account of schizophrenia would be incomplete without the accounts of the lived experience of sufferers and their carers, the bio-medical as well as the psychoanalytic therapeutic models of intervention, and genetics, to inform the work in this area.

Being a member of a family defined by mental illness always made me feel that I had something to write about and share which was 'outside' the average person's experience. Why was it important to share it?

I wanted to understand and help break down the prejudice and stigma felt by those involved. Also, my mother's final wishes were that I care for my sister Celia and I owe this account to both of them.

From my perspective, as the sibling who visited Celia and felt responsible for her care over a period of 40 years, there were some things that were unique to the relationship and distinctive in relation to schizophrenia. What I know now, I did not know at the age of eighteen, on my first visit to Northampton.

From the outset, I felt that I knew my sister well. What I had to learn was how to respond and react to some of the behaviour produced by her schizophrenia, which was often unpredictable and at times aggressive, particularly early on in our relationship. I was always anxious before a visit as it was difficult to know whether or how she would respond to me on a given day, which depended on the different phases of her illness. On some occasions, she seemed symptom-free and the encounter between us and with Peter, my husband, was emotionally rewarding for us all. To use a term more associated with cancer, it did feel at times that Celia had periods of remission.

Celia's letters seem a special case to me, as they appear to be consistently coherent, quite outside of what we typically associate with fractured and disconnected thought patterns. Later on, their paucity of content and lack of narrative fluency are a result of her medication and treatment and life in institutions. Overall, they express her great affection for her family and her longing to see them. What begins as a pleading to Mum and Dad to get her out of the 'bin' and back home is later mellowed to a request for a short holiday there. A tactical move on her part, perhaps realising that to live with the family was unrealistic and not going to happen - ever. What was truly noteworthy about her letters home was that there was no question of her not belonging. She showed in her letters an interest in the lives of family and friends and chose to write about the matters in her life that interested them. Remarkably, Celia's letters were never judgemental. Her letters were at times full of anger towards us, but blame-free. Being non-judgemental in my approach to her and in supporting her was a lesson that I needed to learn and for which I owe her a debt of gratitude.

Then there was a sense of needing to make up for lost time – a necessity to cement the support and deepen the relationship at times of receptivity and interest. It leads us to an understanding of schizophrenia as 'phasic'. What carers and families offer is different during different phases of the illness. In our moments of despair, when all seems pointless, it is important to

understand the nature of recovery in this context. It is not one thing and is
non-linear.

During a phase when Celia showed no interest in writing, and failed over
several weeks to reply to my mother's correspondence, my mother wrote
to a contact at the hospital to ask if her letters made any difference to
Celia. The reply was, "Yes because when she [Celia] feels better she
would hold it against you [Mum] if you failed to write and cut her off."

The continuity and consistency of caring and being interested through
letter-writing mattered here. It was this importance of the connection
between us, Celia, the family at home in Trinidad, and myself as the link
between them, that prevented me ever doubting the need to continue
visiting her. Early on, with Celia in Northampton and me as a student in
London, I had little money for travel expenses. It was difficult at times to
continue. On those occasions, when she was either heavily medicated or
disconnected and psychotic, the experience for me was difficult and
unrewarding. But respite comes in unlikely ways.

Returning from one particularly bleak visit, I stood in thick snow, waiting
for a bus to take me from the hospital back into Northampton to get the
train to London. This was a poorly serviced and under-used bus route and
in later, more affluent, times I would call a taxi to drive me to the station.
Blue with cold and shivering, I accepted the invitation of a local resident
who lived nearby to have a cup of tea to warm up. These were less risk-
averse days. The warmth of that kind act from a stranger has always
stayed with me and a warm cup of tea never fails to deliver what is
required at times of need.

The 'rehabilitation programme' of the 1970s that Celia was subject to
demonstrated her skills at 'independence' but its requirement that she do
more for herself was also a challenge. In 1979, she independently made
the journey by coach to Weymouth to spend a brief holiday with Peter and
me. She handled this well and clearly enjoyed the time with us and the
exhilaration of being 'free'.

It was also during this period that she saw herself as a prisoner and her
letters to me were consistently begging for release. Her clarity of thought
and stability at this time made her aware that she was being judged and
assessed. She recorded in one letter that her behaviour did not match the
requirements of the rehabilitation unit and she was often on the 'bad side'.
Clearly the demands made on her were causing her anxiety and she was
being unco-operative on the ward. These periods of clarity and awareness
shine through in many ways. For example, her realisation that she would

never return to Trinidad to live with her family. She accepted this but still held on to the hope that she might visit.

Throughout her life in institutional care, her schizophrenia never seemed to affect her interest in the family and need for contact. Whether or not it was her medication or the phase of her illness, or both, in the last ten years of her life and well into her 60s, Celia was capable of great joy and tenderness in her dealings with Peter and me. We would laugh together often, though I never saw her cry. The way that she squeezed my hand in the last months of her life told me a great deal about how she felt at a given time. Most telling was, when sick with cancer, in very poor general health and unable to walk, a few months before her death, she so regretted that she could not go out to buy a card for Peter's birthday; something she had always remembered and could previously do.

Celia's Catholic upbringing shaped her outlook and her faith mattered to her. She continued to go to church and receive the sacraments of the Catholic Church for as long as she could. Largely, her various institutional placements allowed for this. The priest who officiated at her funeral knew her well and understood this. Referring to the hymn *Amazing Grace*, sung at her funeral, he talked about how, from our perspective, Celia's thoughts and actions were 'amazing'. In that respect, and in so many other ways, hers was an amazing life.

Voices

C.P.Cavafy (1863-1933)

Ideal and dearly beloved voices
of those who are dead
or of those who are lost to us like the dead.

Sometimes they speak to us in our dreams;
sometimes in thought the mind hears them.

And for a moment with their echo
other echoes return from the first poetry of our lives -
like music that extinguishes the far off night.

Appendix 1

Anthony Luengo: Account of family reunion

We gathered on December 23, 1991, some sixty of us, at San Louis Estate, close to the town of Sangre Grande ("Big Blood"), about twenty miles east of the Trinidadian capital of Port of Spain. To the north of us lay the deep-green mountains of the Northern Range, thick with tropical vegetation, the "high woods" about which Charles Kingsley rhapsodized in At Last! Christmas in the West Indies in 1871. This small estate, some two hundred acres, now belongs to some of the descendants of Michel Julien de Verteuil, including my wife, with whom (along with our two sons) we came from Toronto to be en famille at San Louis.

A de Verteuil, Jacques Alexis, served with the French forces at Louisburg. There, he married Marie DuPont de Gourville, whose brother Michel was part of the migration of planters and their slaves to Trinidad in the last quarter of the eighteenth century. Jacques Alexis was eventually killed during the bloody upheavals in the Vendée during the French Revolution (there were de Verteuils, members of the petite noblesse in western France, on both sides of the conflict). His son, Michel Julien, fled the country to fight with Dutch counter-revolutionary forces, and eventually served under the British flag when Trinidad was taken from the Spanish in 1797. A few years later, at the invitation of his uncle, Michel de Gourville, Michel Julien settled permanently in Trinidad, there founding the island's largest French Creole family. Many of his descendants still live in Trinidad and, increasingly in the last twenty five years, in Canada, the United States, Britain, Australia, and other parts of the world.

San Louis Estate is run by Geoffrey de Verteuil, who lives there with his wife, Marcia, in a simple but comfortable concrete house built high off the ground in typical Trinidadian estate style. Not far from the house, in a lush cacao grove deeply shaded by high forest trees, there is a mound reputed to be an ancient Amerindian midden or burial place. There, Geoffrey, in what some of the assembled family jokingly referred to as the "Sermon on the Mound", spoke to us about the estate's history. Like other cacao and coffee plantations on the island, San Louis has had its ups and downs. At their peak in the 1860-1920 period, such estates had supplied some of the finest cacao in the world to British and European chocolate makers and had provided French Creoles with a comfortable and privileged life. When cacao prices collapsed in the 1920's, however, many estates had to be sold or, like San Louis, heavily mortgaged. San Louis today is not a profitable enterprise for the de Verteuils, but the family holds on to it largely for sentimental reasons. Geoffrey and some locally based cousins do hope, however, to turn around the estate's fortunes by exporting "exotic" flowers to North America and Europe.

A short distance from where we had lunch alfresco, a six-acre grove was filled with these beautiful tropical flowers--red and pink ginger lilies, yellow and red cordyline, golden heliconia. According to Geoffrey, the blooms in this small area yield more revenue than that produced by the cacao and coffee grown on the rest of the estate. If the flower enterprise turns out to be profitable (it just breaks even now), more land will be turned over to it. "If the estate is to survive," he stressed, with a hint of regret, "we will have to go that way."

Estate life in the West Indies for French Creoles, in spite of its many privileges, has seldom been untroubled. Most spectacularly, there was the uprising in San Domingue (Haiti) under Toussaint L'Ouverture in the last decade of the eighteenth century, which overthrew a highly prosperous and brutal plantation regime. This resulted in the deaths of many French planters and sent others fleeing to other West Indian islands. Some of these refugees ended up in Trinidad, where they joined other French Creoles who had started settling there in 1777, migrating like Michel Julien de Verteuil's uncle from islands like Grenada, St. Vincent, Dominica, Martinique, and Guadeloupe. In those islands the planters had been afflicted by "hurricanes, ants, bankruptcy, debts, the decline of coffee cultivation, and soil exhaustion." Thus lamented the father of French Creole migration to Trinidad, Roume de Saint Laurent, a Grenadian planter, in 1777. Through very vigorous lobbying of the then Spanish rulers of Trinidad, Saint Laurent convinced the Spanish to throw open the doors to the beleagured planters of the more northern islands. Part of the deal that he got the Spanish to agree to in the Cedula of Population of 1783 was the granting to each new white immigrant of thirty acres of land as well as sixteen acres for every slave brought to the island.

Babs, a great-granddaughter of Michel Julien and an owner of San Louis estate, was christened Claude-Anne, but acquired her English nickname early on. Like her two sisters and brother, she never spoke French, in fact. By the turn of the century, a hundred years of British rule had virtually wiped out French as the main language of Trinidad (there are still a few speakers of French patois in remote fishing villages). Babs and her three siblings (two of them, Esmé and Rose Marie, now deceased) went to private schools in England, benefiting from the last years of plantation prosperity. She now lives in Palm Beach, Florida, where she and her American husband retired about ten years ago. She still frequently visits Trinidad, to which she feels a deep attachment that is typical of both resident and overseas French Creoles. This is not surprising since Trinidad has been the spiritual and geographical home of this group for the past two hundred years, and remains something of a binding force for the many who now live abroad in places like Miami, Toronto, London, England and Perth, Australia. Palm Beach is not a major destination for French Creoles, but Babs's sister, Betty (Marie Elizabeth), lives not too far away, in Orlando, and assorted nieces, nephews, and other Trinidadian connections reside in significant numbers to the south, in the suburban stretches of Fort Lauderdale and Miami, and almost at the tip of the state, in Marathon in the Florida Keys.

Babs gave a moving short speech that day at San Louis, as she recalled spending some of her early years on the estate(demonstrating how she used to "dance the cacao" to separate the seeds from the pods). She toasted the memory of her long-dead parents, Paul and Valentine, and more recently deceased brother and sister, and confessed that she had been confused when told that the main item on the day's menu was to be "bus' up shut." We were all amused by this: French Creoles of Bab's generation would not have eaten curries in the East Indian manner, with their fingers, using torn pieces of parata bread (hence, "busted-up shirt") to scoop up the spicy meats and gravies. The younger generation is quite comfortable doing so, having assimilated selected aspects of Trinidadian East Indian culture (aspects of the island's African heritage, especially in music and food, have long been assimilated by the French Creoles).

Traditionally, French Creoles married French Creoles. Evelyn Waugh picked up this fact during a brief visit to Trinidad in 1932 and conveyed it in A Handful of Dust through the fictional French Creole Trinidadian Thérèse de Vitré (her surname an anagram of de Verteuil, perhaps?):

> ...there are so few young men I can marry. They must be Catholic and of an island family.

As I looked around me at my wife's many relations that day at San Louis and at later gatherings on Christmas day and in Tobago, the truth of Thérèse's statement still rang true. Among this group, there were de Verteuils married to Rostants (reputedly related to Cyrano's creator), de Verteuils married to Maingots, de Verteuils married to Ganteaumes-- even de Verteuils married to de Verteuils. My wife's first cousin, Derek Rostant, whose mother, Betty, was a de Verteuil, is himself married to a de Verteuil. My brother-in-law, Stephen Cadiz, is also married to a de Verteuil. His mother was born Rose Marie de Verteuil.

Both Derek and Stephen help their cousin, Geoffrey run the business side of the exotic-flower enterprise. This is done very much part-time, for each has a full-time job, Derek as manager of a video-rental store in a suburb of Port of Spain, Stephen as manager-owner of an electric-generator sales-and-service operation based in central Trinidad. Both are die-hard "Trinis." Derek had lived abroad for a number of years, in Ireland at school, later on the Costa del Sol running a disco. Now he is blissfully happy back at home, and often sports a large black umbrella, fully open to protect him against both torrential tropical downpours and the fiercely hot Caribbean sun. This umbrella bobbed cheerfully above us at many of the family gatherings, earning Derek the name of Baron Samedi, the Haitian loa, or Voodoo spirit, that another Trinidadian, Geoffrey Holder, turned with his basso profondo laugh into a figure of demoniacal fun in the James Bond film "Live and Let Die."

Stephen has never lived outside of Trinidad, though he did think about migrating with his wife and three children to Canada a few years ago when he became briefly disillusioned with the political and economic future of the island. Since then, his business has been doing well and he has become politically active. His faith in the island is stronger than ever, and it was at his home that we had the Christmas day celebrations of the Paul and Valentine de Verteuil family reunion.

Picture the prospect: the well-manicured greens of a golf course set in the base of the U of a deep tropical valley; the gentle undulations of the greens punctuated by the shafts of high, thickly foliaged trees and magnificent gold-and-green sprays of thirty-foot tall stands of bamboo; above, an arching, bright-blue sky occasionally streaked with scudding, cottonwool-white clouds. This is Moka Golf course, just north of Port of Spain, as seen from the verandah of Stephen and Suzette Cadiz's house on a sunlit day. Unfortunately, it rained most of Christmas Day, but the festive red-and-white marquee set up in the back garden of the Cadiz house allowed the outdoor lunch to go on as planned. And the heavy rain did nothing to dampen the joyful mood of the occasion.

The Christmas Day menu was eclectic, a mix of local, South American, and--to a North American eye--"traditional" fare, indigenous peas, unripe bananas ("green figs"), and Venezuelan corn-meal pies ("pastelles") jostling the less exotic offerings of turkey, ham, and potatoes. The full meal, prepared in the kitchens of four family members, was listed in a specially printed-up menu:

Suckling Pig
Stuffed Turkey
Glazed Ham
Pastelles
Spanish Rice
Scalloped Potatoes
Stewed Pigeon Peas
Sweet and Sour Carrots
Green Fig Souse
Cucumber Mousse
Tossed Salad
Mocha Pudding
Christmas Cake
Coffee

The suckling pig provided much amusement at the beginning of the day. It had been prepared at a small hotel and ,after unpacking, lay unceremoniously on the kitchen counter, crisp and brown, without the customary apple in its mouth. Its legs were splayed beneath it as if it had been hit by a truck, as so many dogs and other animals are on the island's pot-holed highways. It was quickly carved and the head, now severed, carried aloft at the head of a conga line that snaked its way through the house to the very loud strains of recorded "soca parang," a recent hybrid of traditional, usually religious, Venezuelan-Trinidadian Christmas music and bawdy Carnival lyrics. This mix of the sacred and the profane did not appear to bother anyone. Like other Trinidadians, French Creoles have come to revel in the year-round Carnival spirit that increasingly suffuses all private and public celebrations on the island.

In its own diminished way, our singing and dancing that day mirrored the pre-Lenten festivities that the Catholic French had introduced to Trinidad at the end of the eighteenth century , plantation masquerades that were soon mimicked and eventually transformed by African slaves into the street bacchanal that became the island's carnival. French Creoles like the de Verteuils are now very active participants in the street celebrations, "playing mas'" in multi-racial "bands" costumed according to historical, geographic, and other themes. One is not, however, to imagine the French Creoles moving directly to the streets from their private masquerades: in a transitional period in the 1920's and 1930's, they celebrated carnival in small groups on the open backs of moving trucks from which they gayly threw paper streamers and confetti of many colours onto the pressing mass of black revellers below. Those days of aristocratic elevation above the crowd are now long gone.

The Christmas day celebration at the Cadiz home took up the better part of the day, beginning around noon and ending around nine that evening. In between, in addition to much drinking and spontaneous outbursts of dancing and singing, the lunch took place under the marquee and several speeches delivered in semi-formal fashion (often interrupted by loud, good-natured heckling; Trinidadians are uncomfortable with formality). In one of these speeches (the least informal of them), Bill Cadiz, who has lived in the Florida keys for nearly thirty years, pleaded for more regular communication among increasingly scattered family members. For luncheon entertainment, a group of the "youths from foreign" (mainly teenage and slightly older first, second, and third cousins who live abroad) sang two humourous pieces, one a rap song detailing the arrival of Michel Julien de Verteuil in Trinidad and highlighting events in the family history, the other a random catalogue of island features to the tune of "The Twelve Days of Christmas" (one local beer, six "bus' up shut," and ten potholes among them). An overiding theme--if one could be isolated amidst the effervescent hubbub of chatter, semi-formal speech-making, loutish heckling, and North American accented singing by the younger generation--was that family mattered and that, because of its long association with the family, Trinidad mattered too. The island has for two hundred years provided a geographically defined ground of meaning for the de Verteuils. The pervasive hope on Christmas day 1991 was that the family connections would remain strong even as the Trinidadian context for them becomes increasingly tenuous.

Could such a family reunion occur with equal intensity in, say, Toronto, Fort Lauderdale, or Alburquerque, places where some of those present now live and some even born? In the midst of all the joy, I had to wonder.

ANTHONY LUENGO, June 1992

Appendix 2

St Ann's Psychiatric Hospital, Trinidad (Source: *The Northerly, Issue 4, 2010. Ed. Gillian Henderson*)

History of its establishment

The first available evidence of official concern for the mentally ill in Trinidad was the passing of an ordinance in 1844, for "the safe custody of insane persons charged with offences, and of persons suspected to be insane". The ordinance authorized the keeping of such persons at the Royal Gaol, which was of course less than ideal.

A major step was taken in 1858, with the opening of the Belmont Lunatic Asylum on Belmont Circular Road. However conditions at this asylum remained primitive, as the supervising medical officers at the time did not have special training in the treatment of mental illness.

A major improvement came with the 1882 appointment of one Dr. Seccombe, an England-trained specialist, as Medical Superintendent. Under his stewardship, trained head attendants were appointed, and plans for a new, larger institution were prepared.

J.H. Collens, in his 1886 work "Guide to Trinidad: A Hand-Book for the use of Tourists and Visitors", devotes a short section to the Seccombe-led Belmont Asylum in his chapter "Hospitals, Prisons, Asylums and Homes". He notes the humane conditions in place at the mental hospital, with no mechanical restraints used on the patients. He also mentions a recreation hall, where amusements and concerts were regularly provided.

Nevertheless the asylum was at this point overcrowded. Having originally been designed for 80 people, by 1885 there were over 300 patients. Dr. Seccombe's plans for a larger institution were not fully realized until 1900, when the new spacious St. Ann's asylum, the building we know today, was finally complete. At its inception there were over 400 patients, so its construction came not a moment too soon!

Design

The St. Ann's asylum was built in the form of a number of separate pavilions, rather than all under one roof, which would have made it different from the typical British asylum design at the time. In British asylums, patients were all housed under one roof, but then separated into distinct wings.

The pavilion style was quite possibly a reaction to the tropical climate, since cross ventilation, seen as essential for a 'healthy' environment, and especially so in the heat, was a lot easier to achieve in separate pavilions. There are records of an early 19th-century hospital (possibly an asylum) built in Kingston, Jamaica in the form of pavilions, and this perhaps provided the prototype for St Ann's.

The pavilions would have also been used as a method of separating different types of patients. The norm everywhere by the mid-19th century was to have men and women separated, and there were also separations by 'class' (i.e. whether you were dependent on the state or could afford to pay for a better standard of care and living conditions) and by behaviour (e.g. disturbed, quiet, semi-quiet, chronic, acute etc.)

The siting of the hospital, outside of the centre of town and raised on a hillside, would have been typical - the idea was not only to keep disturbed people away from the general population, but also to give them pleasant natural surroundings, good views, and healthy air, which were all seen as conducive to a cure.

20th century developments

Dr. Seccombe continued as Medical Superintendent at the new facility until 1908, when he retired. It was agreed by all that under his regime, with the help of his assistant, Dr. Rake, the institution had been brought to a high level of efficiency.

Following Dr. Seccombe's retirement, there was a series of Medical Superintendents including Dr. Samuel, Dr. Vincent, and Dr. Smith. The first Trinidadian to be appointed Medical Superintendent was Dr. E.P.L. Masson, in 1948. He was succeeded by his longtime assistant, Dr. L.F.E. Lewis, and then by Dr. M.H. Beaubrun. All three doctors had been trained at the Maudsley Hospital in England.

The title of Medical Superintendent was eventually changed to Psychiatric Hospital Director, perhaps around the time that the building ceased to be known as the "Lunatic Asylum" and instead became the more politically correct "Psychiatric Hospital". Dr. John Neehall, also Maudsley-trained, was appointed Acting Director in August 1971.

Acknowledgements: Many sources were used for the above, as information is quite scant on the psychiatric hospital, perhaps due to its sensitive nature. Thanks to Adrian Camps-Campins for researching the issue and lending us the J.H. Collens book, as well as providing the picture. Thanks to Sister Catherine Bernard of the St. Ann's RC Church, who provided a booklet on the church which also contained valuable information on other St. Ann's landmarks, including the hospital. Thanks to Dr. Leslie Topp, expert on the architecture of mental hospitals, who gave her thoughts on the design aspect.

Appendix 3

Mental Health Policy Matters

1960s General Situation: Lack of information to parents and confusing messages from Celia's doctor in Trinidad and her doctor at St Andrew's Hospital, England.
The Oxford Regional Board's continued financial support for Celia at St Andrew's (a private hospital) is no longer guaranteed.
1961 Mother writes to Father Philip (parish priest known to Celia), appealing for help to find someone to visit Celia, "who could help her get over her loneliness and feelings of abandonment and be a <u>link</u> between her and me" (a forerunner of the "befriending" scheme now currently practised by mental health volunteers).

1962 Electric Shock Treatment is recommended as a therapy for schizophrenia. Celia has two courses during the period 1961-1962. Mrs Doreen Harding, a former mental health nurse, begins to visit Celia on a regular basis and becomes the family life-line with Celia until her death in the early 2000s.

1970s – 1980s A fundamental change in Celia's status at St Andrew's. Northamptonshire Area Health Authority is no longer prepared to pay for National Health Service patients at St Andrew's. There is a request from the hospital for substantial fees as a private patient.

Celia is moved to the John Clare Behaviour Modification Unit in St Andrew's with a view to 'rehabilitation' and 'care in the community' outside of hospital. This was part of a policy change in the treatment and care of the mentally ill, aimed at both cost-cutting and providing a more socially humane environment.

Celia leaves St Andrew's to go to Moray Lodge sheltered accommodation on a 'pathway' to living independently. She is maintained by the National Health Service and Department of Social Security until her death.

Celia is, briefly, living in the community in housing shared with another patient.

1990s Attempt at independent living fails and Celia returns to Moray Lodge. Celia has some success on a 'new' drug, Clozaril, and seems free of her voices. Plans are afoot to have her live in a newly-built National Schizophrenic Foundation house with 24-hour care.

Celia suffers a mental and physical collapse and goes to St Crispin's Hospital for medical attention.

2000-2012 A settled period begins with the transition and move to NSF Lindsay House. Celia shows a good response to Clozarill though the side effects of the drug are manifest. Celia shows a gradual improvement during her long stay in Lindsay House. She enjoys the stability of a settled environment until her diagnosis of lymphoma in 2005.

Bibliography

Allan, Clare, 2006: *Poppy Shakespeare*. Bloomsbury, London

Filer, Nathan, 2014: *The Shock of the Fall*. Borough Press, London

Frith, Christopher and Johnstone, Eve, 2003: *Schizophrenia: A Very Short Introduction*. Oxford University Press, Oxford

Goffmann, Erving, 1968: *Stigma: Notes on the Management of Spoiled Identity*. Penguin Books, Harmondsworth

Hawkins, Margaret, 2011: *The Story of My Sister's Reawakening After 30 Years*. Conari Press, San Francisco

Laing, R.D., 1960: *The Divided Self: A Study of Sanity and Madness*. Penguin Books, Harmondsworth

Laing, R.D. and Esterson, A: 1964, *Sanity, Madness and the Family*, Penguin Books, Harmondsworth

McCloskey, Molly, 2011: *Circles Around the Sun: In Search of a Lost Brother*. Penguin Books, Dublin

Rice-Oxley, Mark, 2012: *Underneath the Lemon Tree: A Memoir of Depression and Recovery*. Little Brown, St Ives

Saks, Elyn. 2007: *The Centre Cannot Hold, a memoir of my schizophrenia*. Virago Press, London

Taylor, Barbara, 2014: *The Last Asylum: A Memoir of Madness in Our Times*. University of Chicago Press

Winnicott, D.W., 2005: *Playing and Reality*. Routledge Classics, Abingdon, Oxford

Bibliography

[faded and illegible text]

Acknowledgements

My thanks go to Irene, a friend from my distant past, whose prompt to 'write it down' first started me on this journey as early as 1982.

To Mark McCrum, whose writing master class I attended two years ago, who helped me believe that it was possible. His mentoring and editing has contributed enormously to this final cut.

To the author and fellow Trinidadian, Lawrence Scott, for finding the time to engage with the work, and for his informed written response to it.

To other family members for their suggestions and comments along the way, particularly my sister Rosie for helping me remember with more accuracy. Mostly, I am indebted to Peter, who is at once my most demanding and supportive critic. This, together with his forbearance and typing skills, has meant more than he could imagine.